Praise for *Tea...*

Real, raw, and unapologetic, ... reminder that true teaching is ... the little things we do, every day, to connect with and transform the lives of our students

—Alex Kajitani, Speaker, author, and California Teacher of the Year

I know a lot of educators—like tens of thousands of them—and CJ is in my top five most favorite. Why? Because he cares about kids—all of his kids—and does whatever it takes to make them feel special, give them access to the curriculum, and help put a smile on their face. He shows up every single day with that mission in mind. *Teach Your Class Off* is like no other book you've ever read, and I guarantee you're going to learn new strategies, laugh, and probably even cry at some of the stories—but you're going to be a better teacher because of it. Ten thumbs up!

—Adam Welcome, Educator, author, speaker, consultant

There are two types of teachers: those who simply transmit information and those who facilitate transformation. CJ Reynolds is the latter. He understands the importance of reaching the mind through the heart. This book is a must-have for anyone who wants to do the same.

—Dr. Dharius Daniels, Author of *Relational Intelligence*,
lead pastor, Change Church

The public school landscape is an obstacle course with a growing population of teachers who face naive optimism, savior complexes, or burnt-out disconnection. Reynolds shares a very honest and insightful depiction of his journey to the core of what all students and teachers can achieve despite the roadblocks. Centering relationships, communication, and joy, he has created somewhat of an "unmodel" for meeting a universal set of needs in the classroom and beyond.

—Aja Graydon Dantzler, Recording artist
(Kindred the Family Soul), writer, and parent

Reynolds exudes teacher-of-the-year qualities on every page and through every story. This book is an essential introduction for any teacher looking to connect with their students through transformational relationships.

—Kayse Morris, The CEO Teacher®

CJ Reynolds is an educator who has his finger on the pulse of pop culture, pedagogy, and the changing demands of the much-needed teacher workforce. In *Teach Your Class Off*, Reynolds goes through practical, pertinent advice for educators . . . especially young educators who want to create passionate, mission-driven students.

—Don Wettrick, StartEdUp founder, podcast host

In a time where education is overcomplicated and underfunded, teaching is overscripted and underinspired, and learning is overassessed and underFUNded, this book will leave you with a thousand kinds of awesome! CJ gives "student centered" fresh meaning, reminding us all that we can inspire and influence students to be "kindness warriors," and that even teachers with district-mandated scripts and little autonomy over the curriculum can create magic and meaningful memories for our students every single day!

—Jen Jones, K-12 literacy specialist, CEO of Hello Literacy, Inc., author of *Get Your Lit Together*

CJ Reynolds is a gifted storyteller. His stories entertain, inspire, and lead to serious reflection on what teachers can do to up their game and ultimately their students' experiences. CJ has dedicated years of his life to giving back to education and educators via speaking engagements, his inspirational YouTube channel, and social media. We finally have his wisdom, tools, and passion wrapped up in a book.

—Tal Thompson, Teacher, family man, speaker, consultant

Teach Your Class Off is spoken truth meets slam poetry meets education! Just like Reynolds, this book is real, authentic, and relevant. Reynolds doesn't try to be anything other than himself, and he helps us look at our students and classrooms a little bit differently. Whether you're searching for inspiration or motivation, this simple, uncomplicated, yet beautifully written book is for you. I couldn't put it down!

—Hamish Brewer, Author of *Relentless*

TEACH YOUR CLASS OFF

Teach Your Class Off

THE REAL RAP GUIDE TO TEACHING

CJ Reynolds

Teach Your Class Off: The Real Rap Guide to Teaching
© 2020 by CJ Reynolds

This book is available at special discounts when purchased in quantity for use educational purposes or as premiums, promotions, or fundraisers. For inquiries and details, contact the publisher at books@daveburgessconsulting.com.

"What Do I Do with the Mad That I Feel?" © 1968 Fred M. Rogers. Lyrics are used with the permission of Fred Rogers Productions.

Published by Dave Burgess Consulting, Inc.
San Diego, CA
DaveBurgessConsulting.com

Library of Congress Control Number: 2020932546
Paperback ISBN: 978-1-951600-10-5
Ebook ISBN: 978-1-951600-11-2

Cover design by Chad Beckerman
Cover illustration by Alloyius Mcilwaine
Interior design by Liz Schreiter
Editing by Reading List Editorial

DEDICATION

To Jenni, Brody, Marley, and my dog, Bentley.
We are the family I always dreamed of.

To David Lee Roth for reminding me
to sail the seas of consequence.

To all the teachers who have dared to be the teacher
they always dreamed of being. Thanks for sowing
the seeds of possibility in your students.

CONTENTS

FOREWORD

Romina

I hated Mr. Reynolds the first time I met him. He was unlike any other teacher I had ever met: caring, personable, and, above all, the most thoughtful person I'd ever had the privilege of knowing and eventually befriending. There's a selfish part of me that doesn't want to share Reynolds with the world. I don't want the world to know how fascinating, genuine, funny, caring, insightful, and overall amazing he is for fear that he will forget about me. That fear quickly vanishes, however, because all he does is care, truly and deeply, about his family, friends, students, and students who become friends. Our bond is undeniable, albeit extremely uncanny. In my graduation speech, I called Reynolds the most important person in my life who wasn't related to me, but now that seems like a lie. This man and his loving family feel like just that to me—a family.

Getting to know Mr. Reynolds was the best and strangest thing to happen to me during my high school years. I say I hated him because I really did. He wanted me to do something I never had done before: open myself up. I grew up suppressing my thoughts and feelings, building a thick skin. Reynolds wanted none of that—he wanted to connect with his students and make his presence known, to show that he cared about us. During high school, we needed someone like him. Plain and simple: high school sucks. But Reynolds made it all bearable. Usually teachers show up, teach you outdated and down-right boring lessons, go home, and forget about you. Reynolds never did that because he couldn't. He created a "safe space" for us in school long before it was a trendy thing to do. He saw us as people, not just ID numbers. I wish everyone had their own Mr. Reynolds. Everyone deserves a teacher who supports you and is in your corner, always.

I have always wondered why other teachers were not more like him. Now more than ever, people are afraid to develop relationships with those they "shouldn't" or "can't." As a fifteen-year-old Mexican girl who grew up in Camden, New Jersey, nothing was more out of my comfort zone than trusting a white male almost twice my age. It took trust on my part to realize that he didn't want to "save" his students. He only wanted to become one with us. He wanted to understand our pain and help us through it.

Mr. Reynolds changed what teachers meant to me. He was proof that you can grow to trust these adult figures we were trained to be scared of. High school would be a lot more bearable if more teachers thought and acted like Mr. Reynolds. If only a few more teachers showed interest in their students—not just in berating us every time we caught an attitude or rolled our eyes—our formative four years in high school would be tolerable.

It was never a matter of convenience for Mr. Reynolds. Although our friendship started when I was in high school, it was after I graduated that we became closer. I spent my eighteenth birthday with his family. His wife, Jenni, baked me a cake and they sang me happy birthday while their three-year-old sat next to me. The following week he took me on my first—and only—driving lesson. I thought we were going to get arrested because I accidentally cut off a cop car. Mr. Reynolds never let it show, but years later he told me my driving made him nervous. When I traveled to London during a college spring break, I walked the city alone listening to the Red Hot Chili Peppers because it's what Mr. Reynolds had done when he had visited the city years before. I also made sure to visit Shakespeare's Globe Theatre, not only because I was fascinated by Shakespeare, thanks to Mr. Reynolds, but because I knew it would impress him. Even during college, I still reached out to him. Regardless of the day or time, I was able to text him with a problem, and he would immediately respond. I don't like talking about myself, but I think the stories that Reynolds and I share are special enough to make teachers

ROMINA'S BIRTHDAY PARTY

want that same connection with their own students. I grew up wanting to be more like him but, more important, wanting to make him proud, to somehow prove that he didn't make a mistake in becoming my mentor.

Mr. Reynolds is the best person I have ever encountered in my life—and that's not an exaggeration. Who else would ask his student from over ten years ago to write an introduction to his first-ever book? I'm really nervous about this. I've written over a dozen drafts of this introduction, hoping the next would be better than the last— not because I want to be perfect, but because he deserves nothing but the best. He always puts others before himself, making sure others feel safe no matter what his situation looks like. It's an honor to call him my mentor. I owe my sanity and existence to the teacher whose classroom I once feared entering—not because I was afraid of him, but because I was afraid of disappointing him. He helped me to be more vulnerable and taught me that it's better to accept myself, with all my flaws, than to change myself into someone I don't recognize. The momentum that he puts forth in this world carries all of us and pushes us to exceed expectations we never deemed reachable or thought we deserved.

Through his stories, I hope you can gather why Mr. Reynolds has had such a positive impact on other teachers and, more importantly, students like myself. This book can show you how one voice transformed the lives of many—students who became teachers because they wanted to "become the Mr. Reynolds" to someone who needs it; students who have his handwriting tattooed on them; students who have their life, thanks to Mr. Reynolds.

To my hero, it's a privilege to have you in my life. You are inspiring, fearless, and humble to such a fault that you can't always see the positive impact you have on those lucky enough to be around you. I am proud of you, of everything you have achieved and will continue to be successful in. It's time to share you with the world.

INTRODUCTION

I teach at an all-boys charter school in West Philadelphia. My students come from homes and neighborhoods that bear little similarity to those found on the safe, tree-lined streets where I grew up. Most of my students come from homes where moms or grandmas hold down two jobs just to hold up their families. Most of my students will be the first in their families to graduate from high school. Every student in my school receives free or reduced-price breakfast and lunch, and many of our students navigate the often-dangerous streets of West Philly just to get to school. It can be a complex environment for students to learn in.

I teach a class called the History of Hip-Hop. I teach lessons based on *Fortnite* and *The Walking Dead*. I listen to Meek Mill and Young Thug, not to be cool but to be relevant. I eat lunch with up to thirty of my students every day during two of the three lunch periods our school has just to give them a safe space to be who they are. I decorated my classroom to be a place where kids want to be. I work as a part of a teaching community. There are no saviors in my class-room, only members of a community focused on what the students need. I've taken kids from the boardroom of VaynerMedia to meet with CEO Gary Vaynerchuk to the jungles of Costa Rica to let them see what exists beyond their block. I've created a YouTube channel to let my students change the narrative that people imagine when they think of black and brown young men from the inner city. We have cereal parties and blow bubbles in the hallway, and we have dance parties for no special reason.

A quick search on Amazon yields over one hundred thousand results for books about teaching. Why throw another title into an already oversaturated market? Because there are no silver bullets in teaching. What works for one teacher does not necessarily work for another. In fact, what worked last year in your classroom might not work this year.

When I started teaching, in one of the poorest and most dangerous cities in the United States, I didn't find many mentors to give me real, practical insight. I couldn't relate to anything I found in books or blogs. Many of the well-intentioned ideas and strategies that teachers suggested seemed impossible for a person with such limited experience and means as myself. Over the years, I've found that I didn't need all of that anyway. My classroom environment is built on just two truths: One, relationships are king. Two, teaching is only ever about the students.

This book was written with my younger self in mind—the idealistic, excited, overwhelmed young person who, after his first day of teaching, wondered what in the world he had gotten himself into. It is not a simple how-to book, but rather a series of stories and lessons aimed at helping *all* educators—whether the ink is still wet on their teaching certificates or they're on the cusp of retirement or anywhere in between—become the teachers they've always wanted to be in the kind of classroom where they wish they'd been a student. Teaching is often overcomplicated. In a world of teacher shortages, scripted lesson plans, and little to no autonomy in the classroom for teachers and students, I think we can do better. We can do better by taking the time to know who our students are and where they come from, what excites them, and the lens through which they see the world.

This is not a book about how to teach in the hood. It is not a book of hard-and-fast rules on how to have an efficient, well-managed classroom. Like teaching, it's just not that simple. This is a book about how I've been able to work as part of a community of teachers and students who have been willing to go outside their comfort zones and have had the audacity to bring silliness, deep relationships, and creativity back into the classroom. This is my story. It's real, no bullshit, and real rap.

1
ALL STUDENTS DESERVE GOOD TEACHERS

Reluctant Student to Unlikely Teacher

Something in my DNA does not like to give up. My father died when I was four, and none of the men on my mother's side of the family graduated from high school. Although I grew up in a solidly middle-class, *Leave It to Beaver*–type community, I attended a vocational high school about thirty minutes by bus from where I lived. My school was in the business of creating workers, not college students, and my very blue-collar family expected me to enter the union as a carpenter right after I graduated. I also didn't like school. I read slowly. I was always in remedial classes or being pulled out for extra help in math or reading. I never read of my own volition. Ever.

But when I start something, even if it's difficult or dangerous, I have a hard time turning back. So, even though my high school was, at times, like a scene out of the movie *The Warriors*, I stuck it out. Just before my senior year of high school, I was asked to be part of a new program where students could test out of high school English classes and take college literature instead. I truly have no idea why I was picked for such a class. *Batman* and *The Punisher* were my typical reading materials. But when I heard my best friend, Gaeson, was taking the class, I thought it would be fun to take it together.

That year, I read the one and only novel-length book I had ever read up until that point, the memoir *Death Be Not Proud* by John Gunther. In the book, Gunther tells the story of his son, Johnny, who had been on track to attend Harvard University when doctors found that he had a brain tumor. The book is incredibly sad, and it made me miss my dad, who had died of the same disease. This was my first experience with the power of the written word. I remember reading a part of the memoir in which the author talks about wishing he had loved his son more. Gunther wrote:

> I wish we had loved Johnny more when he was alive. Of course we loved Johnny very much. Johnny knew that. Everybody knew it. Loving Johnny more. What does it mean, now?
>
> Parents all over the earth who lost sons in the war have felt this kind of question and sought an answer. To me, it means loving life more, being more aware of life, of one's fellow human beings, of the earth.

Something about those words hit my heart hard. I hadn't lost a son, but a father, and this made me wish I had been a better son. The idea that a blot of ink on a page could make me feel something in my heart was a new and radical experience.

After high school, I got a job pumping gas and signed up for community college, mostly because, unlike my classmates or my working-class relatives, all of my hometown friends were signing up. Following the crowd seemed like the best thing to do. It ended up feeling like the worst thing. The professors assigned a ton of reading and expected us to study outside of class. My whole life I had been the well-mannered kid who sat in class and never got in trouble and handed in steady C-level work—not good work, just enough for me to graduate. College was a different animal.

Now I actually had to read the text and study. I had to be an active participant in work groups. I was expected to be an actual student. I started going to the free tutoring my school offered. I needed help with everything—how to take notes, how to study, how to do math. I'd somehow made it through a whole life of schooling without actually learning how to learn.

I tripled down, and, for the first time in my life, I worked my ass off. I would literally say goodbye to my friends in September and tell them I'd see them at Christmas. I listened to one audiobook on the way to school and then read another book in the library when I got to school. As soon as I got out of class, I would head to tutoring. When tutoring was done, I would meet up with my study group. When the library was too full, I would sit in the back of my '87 Chevy van and study there. I was a machine. For the first time in my life, I was figuring out how I learned. I was cutting out distractions and reading, writing, and listening more than I ever had before. I reviewed the class materials over and over again. These were all integral parts of how I grasped what was being taught. This was also my first realization that we do not all learn in the same way. I have kept this knowledge close to my heart in my own classroom and in working with nontraditional students who struggle to find their way in traditional schools.

Becoming the Teacher I Needed

Although I never dreamed of being a teacher when I was a kid, it ended up being the most natural fit for me. As a teacher I get to take the best parts of all of my previous dreams and merge them into one. It was like I'd been gathering ingredients my whole life and hadn't thought of a way to combine them. As a kid, I wanted to be a drummer. I wanted to be on stage and entertain and inspire listeners. But after my band broke up, I went to a monastery and gave serious thought to becoming a priest. My faith has always been an integral part of my life. The idea of walking away from what had been a sometimes traumatic and tumultuous life to sit in quiet contemplation with God and to help those on the fringe who needed love was very appealing. I also spent some time in Zambia visiting very sick children in a hospital. The children lay in their beds day after day with nothing at all to do, watching a TV that showed only static. We tried to bring some light into their lives by blowing bubbles, giving them glow-in-the-dark bracelets, joking with them, and generally just creating some fun in their days, and this experience inspired me. Traveling the world to visit sick children and bring them joy, perhaps by becoming a clown, felt like a dream to me. Teaching has given me a way to take all of my life experiences and ambitions and turn them into my vocation. I've been able to sprinkle magic in the classroom and be a light in people's lives. I grew up as the invisible kid in the back of the classroom. I never once had a teacher with whom I really connected, even though I sometimes desperately needed that connection. I wanted to be a helping hand to serve students and their families. I wanted to bring fun into the classroom. I wanted to help students figure out how they learned and to provide them with opportunities to grow into the young men and women they were destined to be.

But before I relate how I became that teacher, I have a confession to make: I was once an inexperienced and naive teacher who didn't get how the system worked. To be honest, I'm still learning who I am, working through the many implicit biases that I continue to discover in myself. When I first went into teaching, I romanticized what it would be like to work in the inner city. In my heart, I simply wanted to help where help was needed, but I never gave any thought to the interior work I would need to do to be able to teach and connect with my students and their families.

In the spring of 2006, after returning from a short teaching stint at the Macha Girls Secondary School in Zambia, I began looking for my first full-time teaching job. I knew I wanted to teach in the inner city. I wanted to teach in a school on the margins. I wanted to stand like many of my heroes—Saint Francis, Rafe Esquith, and Father Gregory Boyle—with the overlooked and underfunded. But when I began looking for jobs, I applied nearly everywhere in New Jersey—from the rural Pine Barrens to the depths of Camden to the expensive streets of Morristown—to improve my chances of getting an offer.

My first interview was at a middle school in Cherry Hill, a sprawling suburb in South Jersey. It is a fairly diverse community, but some areas tend to lean toward middle and upper class. I grew up just a few towns away, and in high school I spent my nights skate-boarding and eating microwave burritos in Cherry Hill. Most of my friends in the neighborhood were second-generation immigrants whose parents pushed them to do well in school so they could have a lifestyle their parents never had. Whether it was skateboarding, playing in punk bands, or school, these dudes got after it. They were an impressive bunch.

When I arrived for my interview, I was met by the school's entire leadership team. I had a great interview, and I was asked on the spot to come back in a few days to meet with the superintendent and to do a sample lesson. I was thrilled, but a part of me was also hesitant. As I walked out of the building, I noticed an enormous fish tank at the entrance of the school. It was beautiful. The water was clear, and the fish looked expensive. It didn't appear to have any educational value. It was simply calming, fun eye candy. That night I had a hard time getting that fish tank out of my head. Did I want to teach at a school that could afford such an extravagant expense? In fact, did a school like this even need any more good teachers? But on the other hand, who wouldn't want to work there? It was great! As promised, they invited me back a few days later, I presented my sample lesson, and I crushed it. That night, they phoned my house to offer me the job and asked me to come in the following day to sign a contract. What they didn't know was that, the day before I received their offer, I had gone to visit a charter school in the Cramer Hill section of Camden.

The school was only a few years old and was housed in a factory. Half of the building was a middle school, and the other half was an entirely separate high school. Upon my arrival, the building coordinator met me and gave me a tour. The environment was very different from that in Cherry Hill. The hallways were like a maze, and many of the classrooms were tiny. The thing that hit me the most was the fact that every window in the entire high school wing had been boarded up, allowing for absolutely no sunlight in the entire space. After the tour, the building coordinator took me into his office, a small space he shared with the vice principal, who introduced himself as we entered. It was barely big enough to house both their desks. My interview consisted of two questions. One: What was my classroom management strategy? And two: What was it like to teach in Africa? That was it. I answered their questions, and I was told I would hear back from them.

Nothing about this school should have made me want to teach there. The interview was so short I felt like I wasn't really being considered for the job, and no one even mentioned curriculum or students. But I felt like it was the kind of school that might need good teachers. After being interviewed by administrators who did not seem focused on students, I thought I could be a caring presence in a place that seemed void of care. I was left with a dilemma: Cherry Hill was waiting for me to come in and sign my contract, but my heart was pulling me toward the school in Camden. I waited a day. Then another. Still I heard nothing from Camden. I did, however, on the second day get a call from the vice principal in Cherry Hill asking why I hadn't shown up yet to sign my contract. I don't remember what I said, but I was able to hold them off for another day. I told myself that, if I didn't hear back from Camden by then, I would take the job in Cherry Hill for at least a year and then reevaluate the situation.

To my relief, the charter school called me back that night and offered me the job. I called Cherry Hill and told them I was sorry but I was no longer available for the position. Then I drove right over to Camden and signed my contract.

In the five years I taught in Camden, I saw a lot and experienced a lot with my students. The fights were brutal and many. Several of my students were killed on the community's violent streets. Teacher turnover was overwhelming, and student buy-in was difficult, to say the least. The upside was, of course, the kids. I had the honor of being a trusted confidant for many students who had stories they needed to share. Like the student whose mother always wore her hair down because the student's father had attacked her mother with a fork and left her scarred. Or the student whose roof leaked because the previous summer her father had shot a gun at her and her brother as they ran up the stairs. The bullets missed them but put holes in the steps and the roof, so every time it rained the water would come through the punctures, the puddle in the upstairs hallway serving as a reminder of their dad's unpredictability. Or the girl whose boyfriend was shot down just after finding out she was pregnant, leaving the young mother wondering what to do next.

When I say I was honored to hear these things, it's not because I liked hearing about my students' tragedies. It's because those kids could have gone to anyone—a friend, parent, coach, or counselor—but they chose me. Still, the stories were a heavy cross to bear. How do you go from a young person showing you the scars on her arms from cutting herself to teaching about *The Odyssey*? Over the years I've become more adept, but in those early years I didn't know what to do. Those stories would often leave me feeling like I had no right to be in that classroom. These kids needed more than me. How was I supposed to help them when the system didn't care? But I was wrong. I was wrong to think I needed to fix anything. I was wrong to think I was merely dealing with broken students trying to navigate a broken system. And I was wrong to think these problems were unique to those living in neighborhoods like the one where I taught.

Over the last few years I've had the opportunity to meet thousands of teachers through social media and at conferences all over America where I've been asked to speak. If you've ever met me in person, you might have noticed not only how much I love meeting people and telling stories, but also how much I enjoy asking questions and hearing other people's stories. The latter has been life changing for me. Stories from teachers at schools in neighborhoods that look completely different from mine have shown me that we are not all that different.

I was too foolish to realize when I was a young teacher but I've since learned from my many conversations with educators that every teacher and student is fighting a battle no one else knows anything about. As I sat in professional development sessions and had drinks with colleagues late into the night after the conferences had ended for the day, I realized that teachers from some of the richest schools I've ever heard of were working with students who were struggling with pain and heartache and loss just like my kids were. Kids who cut themselves, not because they didn't have enough but because they felt the need to be perfect. Kids who'd lost friends, not to gun violence but to suicide. Kids whose parents weren't around, not because they were locked up but because they chose their careers over their children.

Teaching isn't just about uploading information to your students that they'll need to know on the big test or in the "real world." It's about helping students understand how they learn. It's explaining that being different isn't weird or wrong but is instead what makes a person unique. It's helping kids lean into who they truly are and how they operate and celebrating their individuality. As a kid, I never felt that I could even express, much less celebrate, my individuality. I know my parents and my teachers cared about me; I just don't think they knew how to help me be a better student and lean into my unique self. Even though it was hard, I'm so grateful for that struggle because it has allowed me to understand what it's like to be different. Knowing that people can learn, grow, and express themselves in many different ways has given me an edge as a teacher. No matter what grade or subject you teach or what neighborhood you teach in, it's important to get to know your students. How do they learn? What engages them? Why do they struggle on tests? Why do they want a bathroom pass as soon as it's time to read? In getting to know your students, you will gain insight into parts of them that they don't even know about yet. You can then help them to decode themselves and celebrate instead of self-deprecate.

REAL RAP:

STUDENTS DESERVE GOOD TEACHERS

So how has my career as a teacher led me to write a book? Because I remember. I remember what it was like on my first day in my own classroom in Camden, when I heard that rush of kids coming down the hallway and I thought, "What in the world did I get myself into?" I remember what it was like when I had classroom management issues and couldn't figure out how to get kids to stay in their seats, to stop throwing things at one another, to become engaged in their own learning. I remember being anxious to build connections and relationships with students and unsure how to connect the content I was teaching with the world my students were coming from.

That first year I was hard-pressed to find any books about teaching that I felt spoke to me or that told the hard truth about what it was like to be in the classroom. Most books about teaching felt like they were written by folks who had never actually taught or who had taught for five minutes and then written a book about it. I didn't want that. Instead, I was looking for real rap. "Real rap" is a phrase my students use to describe a person speaking their truth in a matter-of-fact way. It's the truth, no bullshit. I wanted to know how real teachers were getting down in their real classrooms. How they were lighting kids up. How the teachers who came back year after year were making connections with students, parents, and fellow faculty. How, in schools without monetary means, these teachers were able to make something from nothing. This is the reason I started my YouTube channel, *Real Rap with Reynolds*, in 2016. It was a way for me to share what I was doing in the classroom, it gave my students a way to communicate their stories, and it offered other teachers a chance to see what school is really like in the West Philly classroom where I currently teach. I wanted to create a safe space for those in education and those thinking about becoming teachers to hear from teachers and students what it is like to teach and learn in our school. My Facebook group, Real Rap with Reynolds Teacher Talk, was created to give new and veteran teachers a place to share what's happening in their classrooms and to collaborate with like-minded individuals who are tired of the status quo that so often makes school so dreadfully boring.

I'm writing this book with young Reynolds in mind. I'm writing it for all of the new, soon-to-be, and veteran teachers out there. This is the book I wish had existed when I was frantically looking for answers in my first few years when I felt inadequate and alone in my classroom. Teaching is one of the most important and underappreciated jobs in the world. Our students deserve educators who are excited to come to work. I commend you for taking the time to read a book like this and to fill yourself up so you can take whatever ideas it inspires in you back to your own school community. This book is for you.

The Challenge of Creating
a Classroom Culture

*C*reating a positive and exciting classroom culture can seem daunting. Kids can be lazy, tired, ungrateful, and uninterested. And? I felt the same way when I was in school. School sucked every day, and I showed up because my mom didn't play and because I liked my friends. I never had a single teacher who ever tried something awesome. To be fair, I don't blame them. They had to teach apathetic teenagers who would have rather made bowls in woodshop for smoking weed than focus on academics. But when students and teachers want opposite things from their time in class and no one wants to budge, everyone loses. As a teacher, I realize how it can feel to be vulnerable in class, to put yourself out there and pour your heart and soul into a lesson only to have it kicked about by an ungrateful group of students. I also know what it's like to win.

To create a lesson, class, trip, or project so ridiculous you think the kids will definitely go home and tell their parents how you're wasting their time and then their folks will definitely call the principal, which will of course lead to your immediate termination, only to find that it's the most popular and enduring lesson of the year.

What should a teacher do? Should they live, as Henry David Thoreau put it, "lives of quiet desperation"? Hell no! Make your class the best, and look for the kids whose fires you can pour gasoline on! Magic is contagious, and miracles happen. Find other teachers to be awesome with. Make your class the loudest, most wildly engaging space anyone ever walked into. In the end, what's the worst thing that could happen? No one's going to catch on fire. Get after it, Teach! Try something new for the kid who has been waiting all year for you to do something that will grab his attention. Be the teacher you always wanted and needed, and watch your kids, or most of them, come alive.

In this next section, I want to share with you some of my favorite ideas that my students and I have come up with over the years, ways that we've been able to take ordinary lessons and sprinkle some magic on them to make lessons that are irresistible. I heard it said once, "We all know you can lead a horse to water, but you can't make him drink. But what you can do is make him thirsty."

Putting Students in the Driver's Seat: Project-Based Learning

In my first year of teaching, Camden was considered the most dangerous city in the country. The school was housed in an old factory that had no windows in any of the classrooms. We had no money, and the only supplies we ever received at the beginning of the year were a few Expo markers and enough paper to make a thousand copies per teacher. Any teacher will tell you that a thousand copies is barely enough to print all of your syllabi and parent forms in the first term, let alone everything you need to print for an entire school year.

The students that year were an interesting combination. About 60 percent came from homes that spoke English as a second language and the other 40 percent were African American. Most of them grew up in Camden and came to our charter school to avoid the local high schools. When I started teaching, I didn't know what project-based learning was. All I knew was that my students hated sitting still in rows and fell asleep when we read, and I needed to find a way to engage them in learning.

The year before, as a student teacher, I had spent two weeks writing lesson plans that I thought would be epic for Black History Month. We would watch and then break down Martin Luther King Jr's "I Have a Dream" speech. Afterward we would write our own persuasive speeches that the students would present in front of one another. I had done an abbreviated version of this lesson while student teaching, and it was an absolute hit. The lesson would help me check off a ton of core curriculum boxes and would have the students diving deep into one of the best speeches ever written. I excitedly brought my idea in on Monday and told the students what I had planned. I slid in the dusty VHS copy of MLK's famous speech, and no more than sixty seconds in, hands started going up. "Reynolds, do we have to watch this?" "Can I go to the bathroom?" "I need a drink." "Can I go when he gets back?"

It didn't take me long to realize that this lesson was going downhill fast, but I thought if I just pressed on a little longer maybe I could win the kids over. I made sure to show my excitement. I made sure that the kids knew why we were doing it and what the cultural relevance was. It just didn't matter. No one wanted to hear it. It was boring. After two arduous days, I gave in. All teachers know that class time can quickly become NFL time. The game clock might say you have only two minutes left, but, man, those two minutes can feel like two hours. Worst of all, I didn't have a backup plan. This was a two- to three-week lesson. If I did end up scrapping it, what would I do next? I sat in front of my class after the second day of sleeping kids and endless bathroom passes and asked, "If you don't want to do this, then what do you want to do?" I didn't realize it at the time, but this was the best question I would ever ask as a teacher. Why hadn't I asked my students what they wanted to do before?

The kids told me they didn't want to write persuasive essays. They wanted to *do* something: "Like a project or something, Reynolds. Something cool. Like with music or poetry or something." That night I went home and tried to figure out how to marry what the kids wanted with what I knew I needed to cover that year. In the case of my Martin Luther King Jr. project, it was persuasive essay skills, speaking and listening skills, and learning how to work together in groups. I don't know where it came from, but I got an idea that night that I would pitch to the kids the next day that would end up being the highlight of my first year in the classroom. In fact, it's still one of my favorite things I've had happen in my classroom.

The idea was to create a museum in our classroom. Each student would pick an individual or place that was instrumental in the Harlem Renaissance movement. After researching their topics, the kids would work in groups to create an exhibit that would show and tell museum patrons about their chosen artists, musicians, singers, and music clubs. I told the kids that they could literally do whatever they wanted. This project could be as big or insane as they wanted and that I was in the classroom only to help them make their vision come true. I'm not sure exactly what made the kids run with this idea, but they did. For the next two weeks, we transformed our classroom into the Harlem Renaissance Museum. We had no money, but as anyone who has taught in a school with limited resources knows, the name of the game is make something from nothing. Two of my students, Genesis and Yanellis, wanted to make a baby grand piano in the corner of my room, so I visited the Home Depot where I had worked in college and asked my former manager, Nicole Lomba, if

I could have any of the hundreds of cardboard boxes the store recycled every day. She had two of her employees load every available square inch of my 1996 Ford Escort with cardboard. What didn't fit inside the car, we tied on the roof. I looked like Fred G. Sanford from *Sanford and Son* driving into the school parking lot that day.

Being a first-year teacher, I didn't even know if what I was doing was okay. Could I have kids creating instead of just reading and writing? Was I allowed to have students using power tools? Were students allowed to be in the school before and after hours to work on their projects? I had no idea, but I did know that kids were coming into school at seven in the morning with me and staying as late as seven at night just to create their exhibits. Kids would quickly eat their lunch and then come in and continue painting, building, and writing. It was like a dream come true. We would fill our room with the music of Duke Ellington, Josephine Baker, Louis Armstrong, and Billie Holiday. Kids laid on the floor to paint, draw, and sculpt the works of Aaron Douglas and Lois Mailou Jones. And not only did Genesis and Yanellis build a small grand piano in the corner of our room, but they also decorated the walls to look like the Cotton Club. They made small glittery stars that hung from the ceiling and even inserted an electric keyboard into their piano so that it would work.

One day as we were working, creating, and laughing in our room, three gentleman walked in. I hadn't told anyone what I was doing, and I did not see them walk in. I was standing with my back to the door helping a group of students hot glue their cardboard model of the Savoy Ballroom together. When I turned around, I saw that two of the men who had entered were the CEOs who had founded our school. The other gentleman was a guest they were showing around the building. I quickly said hello and then turned back to my students' project. I was immediately struck with terror. I thought for sure the sight of kids with drills and saws would end in my termination. I mean, one dude was meticulously creating a bust of fashion icon Josephine Baker. My man had the wig and makeup on point like he was getting Ms. Baker ready for a show. After a few moments, the men left, and one of my students, Squeaky, ran over to me. "Mr. Reynolds, did you hear what they said?" My heart sunk. "They said 'This is what a classroom is supposed to look like.'" What?! Are you kidding me? To be honest, not all of my colleagues saw the value in what I was doing. I heard a lot of talk about what a waste of time and effort this project was, mumblings of how we could have better used our time getting ready for the high school proficiency test or helping kids raise their reading level. Maybe they were right. Maybe I could have used our time more efficiently.

But for me it was more important to create buy-in from the students. For two weeks, we were a community of learners, researching and creating together in every spare moment. As a community of learners, we filled the classroom's walls from the floor to the fifteen-foot ceiling with projects. Tables neatly lining the walls displayed art, dioramas, and carefully written essays about folks who had made something from nothing on the streets of Harlem all those years ago. In the corner, a stage made of discarded old plywood displayed the grand piano my students had built. Paintings, busts, music . . . It was breathtaking.

Fourteen years later, I still have students from that year hit me up on Instagram and Facebook or see me in the mall and tell me how much fun that project was. The Harlem Renaissance Museum changed our classroom. The students remember all of the details and talk about how much fun they had learning and being with each other. From then on, getting students excited about what was next was a little easier. It was like we had sprinkled magic on our classroom. Even when I had to do some wack school-required lesson or book, the kids would do it because they knew we would get through it together.

Listening to our students can change everything in the classroom. Asking what they'd like to learn about or what sort of activities they'd like to engage in helps students show up for class ready to go because they know they played a part in creating what's happening there. With this particular project, the students still learned all of the persuasive techniques in our curriculum; they just had a say in how that message was delivered.

Caring for Your Students Out Loud

Creating a classroom culture is also about caring for your students out loud. You need to be the example, so your actions do not go unnoticed. Make your actions undeniable and irresistible. Sparks aren't always noticeable, but explosions are.

If we want our students to be kind, empathetic, hardworking, humble, or courageous, we need to be even more kind, empathetic, hardworking, humble, and courageous than they are. Telling a student to be caring toward their classmates is too ambiguous. Instead we need to show them what that looks like so they can see firsthand what we mean. The next step is to help them bridge the gap between what you did and what they can do themselves. As the old saying states, "I hear and I forget. I see and I remember. I do and I understand." Help your students see so they can do.

Donte's family was in the midst of a difficult time. His parents were having issues, and he and his brother stayed at school late every day to keep from having to go to their grandmother's. Donte had told another teacher that morning that it was his birthday but that no one was doing anything special for it. "He told me he was okay and that he was too old for a birthday party or gifts anyway, but you could tell he felt sad," another teacher told me. That afternoon during my prep period, I ran to the dollar store and grabbed a couple of bags of confetti and a few cans of silly string. My co-teacher, Ms. Younkers, stopped by the supermarket and snagged some cookies and then headed back to school. When Donte walked into class later that day, confetti and silly string rained down upon him, and he was greeted with celebratory screaming. That period, as we read together, we ate cookies and pulled party supplies from our hair. What a gift that was for all of us! Donte got a party, and the rest of us got a glimpse into what it's like to give freely.

Kyle was a student in my eighth-period ninth-grade literature class. Eighth period is always my worst period. I'm not sure why, but it always seems to work out that most of the dudes who cause trouble are in my last class of the day. That means I have a large group of guys who have probably gotten into trouble multiple times during the day and who thus come into my classroom already hating the world because they've been getting an earful from every teacher and security guard all day.

Kyle was the kind of kid who, during his freshman year, would trip over everyone's backpacks when he walked down the aisle to his seat. Sometimes he would successfully land on his feet, and other times he would land on his face or on someone else's desk. While the rest of his class was concerned with looking cool and fronting for each other, Kyle had his own type of front. He was very quiet in class and was always willing to help as well. He was extremely polite and was known in our school as the kid who went around to teachers every day just to see if he could help anyone with anything. "Good morning, Mr. Reynolds. Is there anything I can help you with?" I heard that every day from Kyle.

I noticed that Kyle always covered his mouth when he smiled. He had braces at the time, and I've seen this occur commonly with braced-up kids. But I also noticed that Kyle would go even further and try to hide any joy he felt. One day while Kyle and I were eating lunch in my classroom, I asked him why he tried to look serious all of the time. He told me that, when he was growing up, he was teased for smiling a lot. To Kyle's classmates, being openly happy was not cool. Kyle also had a tendency to lose his temper and he wanted to avoid that, so he hid his smiles in an effort to avoid attention and the teasing it often brought.

As the year went on, I began to notice how Kyle was being made fun of on the low. Kyle abhorred rudeness. If Kyle was in a class and the students were not behaving or were being disrespectful to the teacher, Kyle would often slam on his desk or yell incoherent noises because his anger would not stay contained. His inner Hulk came barreling out, and this was always met with laughter and mockery. Kyle was the kind of kid who was an easy target for others because he was not interested in getting revenge or burying someone or being right. He just wanted to be invisible and get his work done.

I've had many kids like this in my classes over the years—kids who are bullied by tough guys who whisper and wait until the teacher isn't looking to make their move and get an easy, cheap laugh. I don't stand for it. Ever. And my response is always the same. I typically have the student being bullied do an errand for me or I arrange for them to help another teacher for part of the class so I can speak to their classmates. That talk sounds something like this: "Gentlemen, you need to know that I see what is going on with [student]. You need to know that this will no longer happen. He is off-limits. You have two choices. One, use your energy to uplift him and help him to feel a part of our community or, two, be quiet. Anyone who gives him a hard time in or out of my class will deal with me."

I then get a handful of my best students, the guys who have been in similar situations before or whom I've been able to build serious relationships with, and I give them an assignment. Their job is simply to acknowledge that student when they see them. It's as simple as saying "What's up?" in the hallway or at the bus stop. Nothing over-the-top. They don't need to ask them to hang out or talk to them about their day. Their job is to take someone who thought they were invisible and insignificant and make them visible. These small acts of kindness literally change the social fabric of our school. I don't force anyone to be kind or to reach out to students who need it. The students just take my request and run with it. They're the dudes who search for kids who are sitting alone in the lunchroom or are secretly eating their lunch behind the wrestling mats or hiding out in the restroom.

My favorite story of these kindness warriors involves a student named Joe who—for good reason—had a reputation in the school as a tough dude. I'd been building a relationship with Joe for a while and he'd gotten in the habit of eating his lunch in my classroom. One day during that lunch period, someone else was teaching in my classroom. Joe was already in the back talking with me when Kyle walked in the room. The room was dark except for a projection screen in the front of the class that was showing a loud movie. Kyle attempted to duck under the screen and move quickly to the back of the room. However, on his way, he tripped on the computer's charger cable, sending the computer flying across the room, pulling my mounted speakers off the wall, and pushing a pile of papers off the front desk. The movie switched off, and every kid in the class started yelling and laughing at Kyle. Kyle froze. He had no idea what to do. He stared at the floor for a moment and then nervously tried to pick up the papers. In what seemed like a flash, Joe jumped out of his seat and yelled, "YO! Shut the fuck up!" Everyone turned around to see who was yelling at them. Joe continued, "Reynolds said Kyle is off-limits!" It is no exaggeration to say that every kid in that class immediately sat down and did not mutter another word to Kyle. Joe walked to the front of the classroom and escorted Kyle back to my desk and then proceeded to clean up the mess Kyle had made. It was one of the proudest moments I've ever had as a teacher, witnessing someone as cool as Joe standing up to the entire class and then helping his brother out by walking him, in front of everyone, back to a safe space. It was also not lost on me that the students, seeing Joe's anger and concern, stopped laughing immediately—not out of fear or regard for the teachers, but out of respect for their brother.

From then on, Kyle was off-limits, and he grew to become one of our favorite members of our lunchtime crew. Kyle also gained the nickname Don't-Smile-Kyle. Whenever something funny would happen during class or lunch, everyone would look at Kyle and remind him not to laugh. It became a game we would all play to see who could get Kyle to laugh.

As I write this, Kyle is getting ready to graduate from high school. Every year, at least a few kids are hard to let go of. You spend four (sometimes five) years with them, and then they graduate. With some you're blessed enough to maintain some contact, but others you might never see again. Kyle is one of the guys I am preparing myself to miss a lot. Kyle is proof of what students can become if they are surrounded by caring teachers and friends.

From Student to Teacher

The prophet Phil Collins once said, "In learning you will teach, and in teaching you will learn." Sometimes the best thing we can do for our students is let them take the reins and teach the class. By allowing students to prepare a lesson, dream up activities, and present what they know about a given topic or idea, we are preparing them to become leaders inside and outside of the classroom.

Donovan Smalls was always a showman. He was the Ferris Bueller of Camden and a hard dude not to like. His personality changed the energy of every room he walked into. He was the kind of guy who had his locker rigged so that, when he opened it, music played and a disco ball began spinning. It was an instant party at the end of every day. He was also the kind of student who, long after he had graduated, came and helped my wife and me with a birthday surprise for our daughter. After seeing my post on social media, Donovan and another special former student, Reann, drove to our home to help us blow up hundreds of balloons to fill our daughter's room while she was sleeping.

Early one fall, Donovan and a group of four other students took a trip with me to Winslow Township High School in South Jersey. Winslow's drama department was putting on a production of *Little Shop of Horrors.* My mentor while student teaching, Nick Zaccaria—or as the kids called him, Mr. Z—was the technical director and told me he would comp as many kids as I could get to the show. So, Jenni and I loaded up both of our cars and drove down. Winslow Township High School put on incredible plays. While student teaching at Winslow, I was able to be part of the theater community. The students are wildly committed to the productions. They stay late after school and come in on Saturdays to help build sets, set up lights, and be a part of the family. In a number of ways, it was quite different from our school in Camden. For one thing, Winslow had a lot of money to put toward their plays, plus they had built a theater company of dedicated students and teachers who worked together to make the shows happen. Occasionally, students who had graduated even came back to help during the week before the shows opened. From the design to the production value, our night in Winslow Township's theater was more impressive than any theater my high school students had ever experienced. Vines came down from the ceiling at the end of the show. Even the plant, Audrey II, was the prop that had been used on Broadway and required two kids just to operate it! At the end of the show, the Winslow students gave my students a behind-the-scenes tour. It was illuminating for them. They got to see how the scenes were built, how the lights worked, how the makeup was done, and how the scenery changed. It was like being let in on a magic trick.

We ended the night by going back to my house for pizza. As we sat around my dining room table, the kids burst with excitement. From the show to the kindness of the Winslow students to the meager little after-party at our house, they loved it all. As we were preparing to take the students home, a dance party started in our living room. My wife and I joined in, dancing with our infant son, and the kids ended the night with a laugh. It was magical, but as far as I had planned, that was the end of it. As it turned out, I was wrong.

A month or so later, Donovan came to me at the end of a school day and told me he had written a play. Surprised, I asked him what had prompted him to do such a thing. He told me that the night he came home from *Little Shop of Horrors* he was so inspired that he sat down and began writing a play called *Gossip: The Rumor Is Out.* His idea was to create a production he could put on for his friends and family. Over the course of his junior year, Donovan wrote and rewrote the play. He got help from teachers when needed, and by the end of the year he had finished his script and was ready to put on his production. The problem was our school days went until five in the afternoon, and I knew our students would never commit to something that had them staying at school later than that. So, Donovan and I came up with a plan. We would write up a course description and pitch it to the administration so we could create a drama class with the express intention of putting on Donovan's play. I'm not exactly sure what made the school say yes, especially because so many of my previous requests—to take trips, to invite speakers to my class, to use unconventional activities, and more—had been turned down, but they did. The lesson I learned was to keep asking. One of my heroes, Pat Croce, the former owner of the Philadelphia 76ers, famously said, "If you don't ask, the answer is always no."

That summer, just before his senior year, Donovan got to work putting everything together for the play. He paid for almost the entire thing out of his own pocket. I think the school gave us something like one hundred dollars for the production, so Donovan scoured the Internet to find deals on costume pieces and props. When I think back on that summer, I'm amazed at how much work he put into his dream. Not only did Donovan write and direct the play. He created every costume, choreographed all of the dances, designed the sets, and even designed all of the fliers himself. It was an epic undertaking, especially while trying to complete senior year. That September, the administration decided that our class would take place during the last period of the day in my classroom, which at the time was located in a leaky trailer in the back of the school. We made an announcement to the school and had auditions. After we picked the cast, it was game on. Every day during eighth period, Donovan ran rehearsals and worked step by step to make his project come to life.

It's important to interject here that I was merely a facilitator in all of this. I was more like a hired hand than a teacher, which was fine with me. Teaching can often feel like trying to herd kittens. During this class, I was able to play the role of dream facilitator. I ran lines with kids, made sure the lights and sound were working, encouraged the young actors and actresses when they were tired and fed up, helped to build our modest backdrop and props, and was an empathetic ear to Donovan when he needed it.

Sometimes handing the class over to the students and allowing them to be in charge of what and how the class is learning helps them begin to grasp what teaching and learning are really all about. In my opinion, Phil Collins got it exactly right when he said, "In teaching you will learn." Teaching someone else is one of the best ways to build true understanding.

This play was Donovan's first look into what it was like to be in charge—not only of the play but also of the students. He got to see how difficult it was to motivate students after the newness of the year wore off and how painstaking it was to get kids to stick with their commitments. It's hard to stand back and watch students struggle, whether it's with a science experiment, a math problem, or a difficult book, but that struggle is what helps students build perseverance in their academics and in their character. Donovan had never worked so hard on anything in his life, and because he didn't give up, he learned the joy of seeing life's most difficult challenges through.

We made it through the year together. As with every class, there were hiccups. For example, a week before the performance, the cast became aware that the lead actor didn't know his lines at all. We were stuck. No one could possibly learn all of his lines before the show started the next week. The only person who knew the lines and the cues was the man who wrote them. So, along with writing, directing, choreographing, set design, costume design, and running logistics on programs and theater seating, Donovan took on acting as the lead of the play.

The school couldn't find time for us to run through the entire play on the school's stage until the day before the scheduled performance, but when we finally did it, everyone's hard work paid off. On the night of the show, it was evident that Donovan's first play was more wonderful than anyone could have expected. The actors and dancers gave their all on that stage, and Donovan was outstanding in the lead. The crowd response was incredible. So many people showed up that the school ran out of seats. As a result, folks took to sneaking into the gym through the side and back doors just to be a part of what Donovan and his classmates had created. It was another of my proudest moments as a teacher. That year we spent practicing and preparing for the play in my leaky trailer was beyond stressful. So many times, the students wanted to give up, and more times than I can count, I wanted to take over. But we stuck it out. We worked together as a community to make the students' vision come to fruition.

After his senior year, Donovan went to Rutgers University to study theater. He has since received his master's degree and returned to his alma mater to teach in addition to running his own performing arts company, DRAMATiK Academy. He has gone on to write some of the most engaging and exciting high school productions I have ever seen. He is a testament to what happens when teachers get out of the way and hand the captain's wheel over to the students. The greatest gift I could have given him that year was to let him follow his dream, to let him try and fail repeatedly, to help him dust himself off and keep going. The gift I received in exchange was the opportunity to witness Donovan's struggles and his ultimate win. Donovan, if you're reading this, know that I am prouder of you than you know. You are a warrior, and I am blessed to have been a part of your journey.

Sprinkling Magic on Your Classroom

Teaching is often overcomplicated. In my first years of teaching, I would agonize over how to make my class engaging, relatable, educational, and enjoyable while still meeting all of my curriculum standards. A quick Google search yields countless results for lesson plans and ideas on everything from polynomials to scientific method to the proper use of a participle. Starting out, though, I thought I had to re-create the wheel.

I've learned since then that the missing ingredient in most classes is magic. I wanted my class to be the greatest thing any kid had ever walked into. I wanted students to share my excitement about learning and to be pumped to come to class every day. This is especially missing in schools that have moved toward scripted lesson plans and away from classrooms in which teachers have the autonomy to do what they deem important for the students. Teachers who have taken the time to build personal and educational relationships with their students know a lot more about what those kids need than someone who has never met them. I'm blessed to work currently at a school that gives its teachers full autonomy in the classroom. The rules, procedures, and lessons I've created for my literature and History of Hip-Hop classes are completely up to me. That level of freedom can be scary to some teachers while leaving other educators jealously longing for a bit more liberation.

Regardless, I believe teachers can sprinkle magic in even the strictest educational environments through the lessons and classroom environments they create. Whether you're the lead teacher, assistant principal, or classroom aide; you have the power to change someone's day by simply disrupting their daily routine. Let's cut to the chase! Here are some ways that I sprinkle magic on everyday school moments and classroom activities.

Bring happiness to the hallways. Every day as I stand in my doorway and greet the students entering my classroom, I watch the same teachers and kids make their ways to their classrooms. Some slowly walk down the hallway with their heads down, some play fight, some nervously try to remember where they should be, some rush to make it to class on time, some linger at their lockers. It's about as exciting as being a traffic cop who stands at the same intersection day after day, year after year. It's also the perfect place to infuse a bit of fun and silliness into the day. In these five-minute interludes between classes, I love to blow bubbles in the hallway. I have literally *never* seen a student who was not positively affected by bubbles in the hallway. Sometimes they are annoyed at first. I've seen students walk to class and begrudgingly pass through my cloud of happiness while angrily swatting away my efforts at making them smile. But after their second or third time passing my room, when a bubble lands on their shoulder or hits their nose, they become powerless to resist the magic of bubbles.

When closed, the bubble wands I use are the shape of a microphone and are always custom-painted gold because, if Prince had a microphone bubble wand, I imagine it would have been gold. The microphone is a fun way to interview kids as they walk to class. I pretend I'm a local news anchor, and I ask students questions as they pass by. "Excuse me, Mr. Lopez, our viewers are wondering why you're late to class every day?" "Oh, there she is! Ms. Little could you tell our audience what it's like to walk so slow you're on the verge of walking backward?" I guess I could just as easily ask kids to hurry up before they're late to class or remind them that they could potentially get a detention for playing around or being tardy, but addressing regular problems with out-of-the-box thinking puts a little magic in the day. It helps kids to lighten up while still holding up a mirror to what's going on. It's also just a happy surprise and makes what might have been an ordinary day a little better.

Deep Thoughts with Uncle Barry. Barry was a quiet introvert of a student. During his freshman year, he found it difficult to fit in with the rest of the kids in our class. Every day when we write journal entries as our opening activity, most of my students write about football, girls, video games, or times they got caught doing something they shouldn't. A lot of posturing and fronting happens in the ninth grade when you're trying to figure out who you are and what you're about. The last thing most kids want is to stand out. Barry, on the other hand, would shyly but relentlessly write about things he cared about or fantastic ideas that would run through his head. When asked about their favorite thing to do after school, Barry wrote about how he loved to play with his cat. When asked what would be their spirit animal, many students wrote about lions and eagles but not my man Barry. Barry would rather be a dolphin or a unicorn. Barry would often write about inspirational ideas and share how much he wanted the world to be a safe and beautiful place where everyone was accepted and belonged. It's no surprise that Barry's answers got a lot of attention, usually in the form of laughter or teasing. When this happens to a student in your class, you have a few options for dealing with it. You can talk to the student about being mindful of what they choose to share with the group, knowing that what they say could draw negative attention. You can also talk to the class about accepting that student for who they are and threaten to discipline anyone who makes the class an unsafe space for any student. Both of these ideas can work, but I like handling these things another way.

One day after Barry wrote his journal entry, I asked him if I could read it before he read it aloud to the class. He had again written about how wonderful he thought the world was and how he hoped for a world in which we could all live the lives of our dreams. Instead of threatening the class to act properly, I waited until everyone else had read, and then I announced, "Today's journal grand finale will be presented by a young man who is not afraid to speak from his heart. He is more like a trusted uncle than a classmate. He gladly shares his deep and profound wisdom with us daily, and today will be no different. Gentlemen, it is my honor to present 'Deep Thoughts with Uncle Barry.'" Barry then walked to the front of the classroom, and as he began to read, I played "inspirational music" I found on YouTube. I couldn't be more serious in saying that the music playing behind Uncle Barry's words transformed what he was saying. Try it. Take any poem and meaningful selection from a book and read it with the right music behind it, and it will transform what you are saying. Real rap: Uncle Barry got a standing ovation that day after he read. "Deep Thoughts with Uncle Barry" became the way we kicked off class every day after that. The students all took to calling him Uncle Barry, and he became a celebrated member of our classroom, loved by everyone.

I've got a fever, and the only cure is more music. As it did with Uncle Barry's inspirational speeches, music has the power to transform a space instantly. When students are walking in and out of class, play some low-key music in the background to set the vibe for the day. When you're reading a book with your students, play music behind a particularly intense passage to increase their interest. Lean into the music and read with a dramatic tone, and you'll be amazed at the results. When we play review games in class, we play a dozen different versions of the *Jeopardy!* theme song in the background. Trap, hip-hop, trance, low-fi, 8 Bit remix . . . The kids love it, and it builds engagement by just changing up the norm a little bit.

Give your guests a round of applause. If you ever walk into our classroom in the middle of a class period, my students and I will immediately stop what we are doing and give you a round of applause. My students have been instructed to clap for anyone who visits our classroom, from the principal to the school nurse. Why? Because you deserve it, and it's fun. My good friend Ms. Cho has a resting face that just looks angry. "Hey Cho, you good? You look angry?" "I'm not angry this is just how I look." But when Cho gets our standing ovation, even she can't help but smile.

Offer uncommon solutions for fidgety students. One year, on a whim, I made an astronaut helmet out of an old cardboard box, a sharpie, and some pencils for antennae. A student of mine, Marcus, loved the helmet and would wear it during our lunch time. Marcus had a very hard time getting centered in class, especially when we were reading either as a group or individually. One day in class during silent sustained reading, Marcus asked if he could wear the astronaut helmet. I told him he could only wear it if he promised to do his best to focus on his reading. He made the promise, and this fifteen-year-old kid sat in the center of class silently reading his book while decked out in a cardboard astronaut helmet. Like Frosty's magic top hat, our astronaut helmet helped several kids to focus on their reading and writing assignments in class. I have also had the same experience after handing kids eyeglasses with no lenses in them. I tell them they are a special prescription that helps me read and I only share them with a select few kids who might really need them. Every time they work like a charm.

Make collecting papers fun again. All teachers know that collecting papers from your students by walking up and down the aisles of your classroom can look more like a scene from *Tomb Raider* than a simple stroll through a classroom. The aisles teem with trip lines, feet hidden under jackets, backpack straps, football helmets, and crocodiles. To minimize personal injury, I made a Shaquille O'Neal–sized hand out of thin plywood and attached it to the end of a yardstick. Now, instead of walking down the aisles of certain doom, I simply extend my hand on a stick and collect work with ease. The hand also works for gently waking students who have fallen asleep, giving high fives, and, during the right song, waving your hands in the air like you just don't care.

Throw a cereal party. Teachers love pizza parties. And why not? They are awesome, and everyone loves pizza. But man, you've never

THE LEGENDARY
HAND ON A STICK

seen kids get more excited than when you roll into class with boxes of their favorite cereals. Not just any cereal either. It *needs* to be cereal with the least nutritional value. Every kid loves cereal, and the less nutrition it has, the more excitement. You can easily make accommodations for the peanut-free kids and the kids who can't handle regular milk. I will say now that your class has never been as quiet as it will be when you have students shoveling this artificially flavored magic into their mouths. Best of all, cereal is about the same price as pizza. And if even that is outside of your budget, how about a party fueled by Top Ramen? The grocery aisles are full of options for any budget when you think creatively.

Play around with tiny water pistols. I once picked up a tiny water pistol while I was out shopping. I brought it to school without a plan of how I would use it, and then one day while I was in the hallway at the end of the day saying goodbye to the students, I filled up my little alligator-shaped water pistol and hid it under a book I had placed on my arm. I then proceeded to squirt kids in the leg or the arm as they walked by. I also would squirt the water pistol in the air, which made every kid who walked by look up at the ceiling as if it were leaking. This is one of those activities that you need to do to the right kid at the right time. Done right, however, it is endlessly hilarious, and the kids *love* it. Talk about shaking up what you thought could happen in a school hallway. Nothing snaps you out of your norm like a shot of water.

Write on your students' desks with *permanent* marker. One of my favorite ways to get through to students who are having a tough time in life or in class is to write quotes on their desks that they can't easily remove. They can be lighthearted quotes like "You are enough" or "You are perfect just the way you are" or harder hitting quotes meant to cut through the noise, like this favorite quote from Henry Rollins: "If you hate your parents, the man, or the establishment, don't show them up by getting wasted and wrapping your car around a tree. If you really want to rebel against your parents,

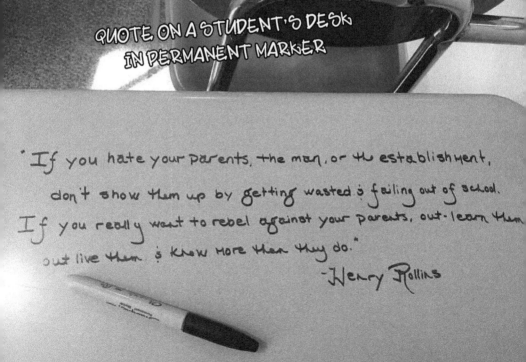

out-learn them, outlive them, and know more than they do." That daily reminder can be more than they get from anyone else. (In case you're worried, permanent marker on school desks is not really permanent. It can be removed with many household cleaners or even with plain rubbing alcohol. It might require a bit of scrubbing, but it *will* come off.) If you'd rather not use permanent marker, you can also get your message across by using chalk markers or writing on tape that's been placed on the student's desk.

Have fun with eyeball stickers. I have a pile of stickers in my desk drawer that have eyeballs on them. I make them myself because, honestly, what manufacturer is going to say, "Aha! I know what the people want! Eyeball stickers!" I use these stickers for one of my best dad jokes. When I see a kid who looks like they might be having a tough day or feeling invisible, I put an eyeball sticker on them and say, "I've got my eye on you." It's both hilarious and meaningful. I just want kids to know that they are seen and cared for. I don't know every kid in the school, and I don't always have time for, as my friend Flounders says, a "heavy, deep, and real conversation," but I always have a moment to put my eye on a kid who needs it.

I have dozens of ideas like the ones I've shared here, each one more ridiculous than the last. Whether it's extending tiny plastic hands out of my sleeves to shake hands, tying toy mice to the end of fishing string and pulling them down the hallway, changing teachers' family pictures on their desks to pictures of me, or using a megaphone to direct traffic between classes, I'm always looking for ways to make someone's day. Wherever my wife and I go, we are constantly looking for new ideas to bring to school. I keep all of these treasures in two suitcases in the back of my classroom. One suitcase is labeled "Weird Stuff" and the other "Weirder Stuff." They are filled with all types of ingredients for making magic in our classroom. Fake mustaches, inflatable lightsabers, masks, puppets, first place medals, confetti, fake money, beach balls, fake flies and ants, bubbles, silly putty . . . It's all perfect for disrupting any average day and making it a bit more magical.

REAL RAP:
YOU CAN CREATE THE CLASSROOM
CULTURE YOU WANT

School can be a dreadfully boring experience. Students trudge from one class to another, and in each one they're expected to sit quietly, sometimes for an hour or more, and passively absorb information that will be on some big, dreaded test in the future. But by just moving the needle a little bit in your classroom, lessons, or relationships, you can sprinkle magic on the day. It's about figuring out what your superpower is as a teacher and then leaning into that part of yourself to create a better experience for yourself and those around you. Really think about what makes you special. Are you great at breaking down difficult concepts? Are you patient? Creative? Funny? Organized? Empathetic? Artistic? How can you use these gifts to make your classroom and school a more enjoyable place?

Being silly is something that has always come easily for me. I have no fear of looking like a fool in public, although this wasn't always the case. I was always funny at home as a kid, but in school I kept most of that to myself for fear of being ridiculed. In college I read *Gesundheit* by Dr. Patch Adams. In that book, Patch says, "The most revolutionary act that you can commit in our society today is to be happy." This statement hit me hard and changed my life. The idea that I could help change the world or at least better someone's day just by being happy was a revelation. I began looking at being funny and happy as a service I could provide for the world. In that same book, Patch also says, "Humor is the antidote to all ills." As a teacher, both of these ideas have given me the courage to be unapologetically myself and to lean into who I truly am as a way to serve others. This isn't about rewriting the curriculum or changing all of the hard work you've put into creating your classroom or your lesson plans. It's not about mimicking someone else's success in the classroom. It's about taking what you already are and turning the dial up to eleven. Putting an eyeball sticker on a student as they walk down the hallway or writing a message on their desk might seem like a waste of time or too small of an act to cause any real change, but I would argue that, in doing such things, you are potentially showing someone who thinks they are invisible that they are seen. This is my way of using my wackiness to let a child know they are important.

BUILDING STUDENT RELATIONSHIPS

Relationships Are King

*I*n my classroom, relationships are king. That came about because of events in my life that shaped who I have become as a teacher. In my freshman year of high school, I walked into my new school's enormous lunch room and stood there with my brown paper lunch bag and looked around for somewhere, anywhere to eat. I knew no one and lacked the confidence to walk up and ask someone if I could sit with them. I wanted to skip lunch all together. The embarrassment and heartache of having nowhere to fit in is soul crushing, especially for young people. I mustered whatever courage or insanity I had and walked up to a lunch table populated by the most enormously tall and muscular kids I had ever seen in my life. Of course, I couldn't just sit down and introduce myself. That might end in me being rejected, which is the second worst thing that could have happened in the situation. (The first would have been being punched by a kid the size of a brown bear.) Instead, I slowly placed a half a butt cheek on the open chair next to them when they weren't looking. Just as I had made touchdown, one of the guys looked over at me with a stare that said, "Any closer and I will cut you." I froze. I looked like I was in a *Jurassic Park* movie and a T-Rex had just spotted me. It seemed like I sat there forever with my fraction of a butt cheek on that chair until finally this bearded, full-grown-man–looking child gave me the nod to let me know I was granted permission to stay.

Fast forward fifteen years or so, and I have my own classroom. My experience in high school stuck with me so much that, when I got my first classroom, I announced on the first day of school that students were more than welcome to eat with me in my classroom during lunch. This proved to be one of the single best decisions I ever made as a teacher. Eating lunch with your kids, whether it be in your room or at their table in the cafeteria, will yield more opportunities to connect with them than any other time. It is uninterrupted face-to-face time to learn who your kids are and what they care about. It's like a reconnaissance mission. You're collecting data that you can then use to transform your lessons and the way you deal with students as individuals. Want to know what everyone is talking about, what the best new movies and television shows are, who broke up, who's being bullied, what the quiet kid cares about? Eat lunch with your students and find out. This time helps me know who I need to check in with because their boyfriend or girlfriend broke up with them, who might not be getting enough to eat, who's struggling to fit in, and what YouTube videos or movies I need to incorporate into my lessons. More than anything, however, it provides me the opportunity to give *all* students a place to belong and allows me to build strong, lasting relationships with my students.

On my YouTube channel, *Real Rap with Reynolds*, I have the honor of connecting with teachers and soon-to-be teachers from all over the world. I have answered thousands of questions over the years, but one that is asked more than almost any other is, "How do you build relationships with students?" Teachers have a lot of apprehension about this topic, and perhaps rightfully so. Every school year brings new stories in the media about a teacher who got a student pregnant or a student who made an inappropriate advance on a teacher or teachers sending unprofessional emails or texts to students. Especially as a new teacher, it can be hard to navigate these waters. A lot of young people entering the profession ask me, "How do I draw the line between friend and caring teacher?" "What do I do if a student doesn't want to have a relationship with me?" "What do I do if a student comes into my room when I'm alone?" The questions go on and on.

Some of these answers are simple. If a student doesn't want a relationship, don't force it. You will not be the messenger for every child. Just stay open in case you are ever needed. If a student comes into your class and you are alone, keep the door open, or better yet, make sure your room is the hangout spot for kids. My room is never empty. That is no accident; it is by design. Nothing attracts a crowd like a crowd. Just having other kids in your room makes students want to be in there, and it makes a student who needs your help, whether with school or with life, feel comfortable coming to see you.

Keeping that line between friend and teacher firm can be a tough one. It comes down to learning how to have difficult conversations. In fact, I think your success in life depends on your ability to have uncomfortable conversations. Want a successful friendship, marriage, band, or business partnership? Learn how to have difficult conversations. When a student oversteps the bounds in our relationship, I lay it out for them plain and simple: "Student, I need you to understand that you are extremely important to me. But don't get it twisted. Your success and education are infinitely more important to me than whether or not you like me. I cannot make myself a part of the equation because, if I do, I won't be able to be straight with you." Some situations, however, are not as easy to figure out.

Your Attention Matters More Than Your Advice

The spring before Joe entered my class, I had promised my friend Ms. Younkers that I would take over the co-taught ninth-grade literature class. I had never had a co-teacher before, but Younkers couldn't find anyone to teach the class and inner-city schools like mine often have a hard time finding qualified special education teachers because they can't afford to pay folks who have experience. That fall I was paired with a first-year teacher who came to our school via Teach for America. My new co-teacher and I were given a class of thirty kids who either were reading between a second- and fourth-grade level or had been identified, officially or unofficially, as a discipline problem.

Joe was a skinny, quiet, angry-looking child. He came reluctantly to class every day and never did any work. He mostly just laid his head down on his desk and doodled on his notebook cover. Typically, when this happens, my first reaction is to squat down next to the student and make sure everything is okay. I recommend always squatting down and never leaning over a student because leaning over a person makes me feel like I'm putting myself in a position of power and control when what I want to convey is a sense of care. I then just check in. "Are you okay?" "Are you sick?" "Do you have smallpox?" If a kid says they're okay, I ask them to please sit up. Sometimes they do, and sometimes they keep their heads down and the struggle continues. Joe kept his head down.

In phase two, I ask the student to step into the hallway. I do this so much that by mid-year my students mock me by saying, "Would you please step in the hallway? You are not in trouble." They are right. I always politely say, "Please step in the hallway. You are not in trouble." I make sure to say it this way because kids are far more likely to comply if you let them know on the front end that they are not being kicked out or reprimanded. What I'm really doing is taking away the student's audience. Some kids act a fool because their friends are watching and they don't want to look like a punk. Other kids want to act like they don't care and try to show how tough they are by refusing to look you in the eye, even if you're just trying to help. Getting them away from their classmates' gazes decreases a lot of those behaviors.

Once we're in the hallway, I ask, "Did I do anything to upset you?" I *always* ask on the front end if I did something wrong because it throws kids off. Students usually expect to be reprimanded for their behavior when they're taken out of the classroom, so they're caught off guard when an adult allows for the possibility that the *adult* did something wrong. I'd say about 90 percent of the time the student acknowledges that I didn't do anything wrong and that they made the wrong choice. Being alone in the hallway, we now have a brief uninterrupted moment to handle the situation. About 10 percent of the time, a kid does have a problem with me. Maybe I didn't call on them during a test review or they asked a question and I didn't hear them so they thought I was ignoring them on purpose. Maybe they took a joke I made the wrong way. Whatever it was, I now have the opportunity to explain myself and to apologize. Apologizing often throws kids off as well. I mean, how often do adults apologize to kids? After I model what it looks like to explain oneself and ask for forgiveness, we reenter the room and get back to work. Once we return to the classroom, something has changed between that student and me. In those few moments, I'm able to give the student a glimpse of my sincere concern for them, to demonstrate that I'm willing to be wrong, to prove that I have more interest in them being heard than in being right, and to show them that they're not invisible.

Joe responded to none of this. Here's an example of the kind of exchange we'd have:

"Hey, man, did I do something to upset you?"

"No."

"Is there something I can help you with?"

"No."

"In that case, I'm going to need you to sit up and participate."

Silence.

"Joe? Do you hear what I'm saying? I'm open to anything you might be thinking."

"I'm not thinking of anything."

This went on for more than a month. Sometimes Joe would meticulously complete his work in his signature beautiful handwriting, and other times he was head down and doodling. I wasn't sure what to do, but for some reason, the situation reminded me of a time I got bullied in tenth grade and how my mom helped me solve my bullying problem.

In tenth-grade history, a guy named Tom sat in front of me. Tom was bigger than most of the kids in my class, and he knew it. Every day when Tom would walk into history class, he would first punch my friend Gaeson in the arm and then punch my lunch bag. It was a lunch that my mom made for me every day. Nothing fancy, just a PB&J, a Tastykake, and a napkin, with my name written neatly on the front. Every day, though, Tom would come in and crush it all, and I'd be eating flat PB&J for lunch.

One night, I went home and told my mom about this. I told my mom about most things that happened in my life. The next morning, I came downstairs for breakfast and found *two* brown-bagged lunches on the kitchen counter. One said "CJ" and the other "Tom."

"Mom, what's this?"

"Oh, I made two. When you walk into class today, I want you to put that one on Tom's desk and tell him it's from me. Let him know there's a note for him inside."

I still don't know why I listened to her. I mean, giving a bully a lunch your mom made for him is like giving a kid permission to make mom jokes until the end of forever. I secretly hoped my mom had filled the lunch bag with nails so Tom would stab himself when he punched the bag and he would never mess with me again. I wasn't so lucky, but I was even more surprised at what happened next.

I walked into class and placed the bag on the corner of his desk. "Here, my mom made me bring this for you. She said there's a note inside for you too." He didn't know what to do. I watched him open the bag and read the note quietly to himself. He then turned around in his seat and didn't crush my lunch. In fact, he never touched my lunch again.

That spring my mom came to school for an open house, the kind of thing where the parents come to see their kids' projects and meet with their teachers. My friends and I would show up to just hang out and walk the halls. While I was waiting in the hallway outside of my math class, Tom walked up to me and asked if my mom was with me. "Of course, she is. She's down the hall in the geometry room," I said. Tom walked to the end of the hall just as my mom was walking out of the classroom. I watched him introduce himself. I couldn't hear what he said, but as he was talking, my mom opened her arms and hugged him. He hugged her back. My mom died in 1998, and I never asked her what she wrote on that note or what she and Tom talked about at the end of the hallway. The exact words weren't important. It was the act that was important—the act of noticing someone who until then had gone unnoticed, the act of meeting fury with kindness.

So, after a month or so of Joe sitting with his head down, being belligerent with my co-teacher, and refusing to do work or even being willing to sit up straight, I gave him detention. However, his detention would not be served after school as most detentions were; it would be served in my classroom every day for a week.

My classroom, almost since the beginning, has been the place to be during lunch. An extremely eclectic group of students gathers there. More than anything else, it resembles the Island of Misfit Toys from *Rudolph the Red-Nosed Reindeer*. I try to provide a safe place where anyone can hang out during lunch instead of eating in our lunchroom. The result is a wild mixture of kids who play Pokémon and Magic: The Gathering, kids who have cyphers in the corner and give each other feedback on their wordsmith skills, kids who hold court and talk deeply about last night's episode of *The Walking Dead*. Groups of athletes talk sports and get hyped for that day's game, while one kid makes paper dolls and puppets at a desk. And some dudes just need a quiet place to listen to music or watch Netflix.

When Joe came in that week for his detention, I told him he could sit anywhere he wanted, but that I was going to sit with him, though he didn't have to talk to me. He could just eat his lunch in peace and I would do all the talking or just ask him questions that he didn't need to answer. On the first day, Joe walked into class and sat in the back corner.

"Hey, man. I'm glad you're here. Feel free to eat your lunch while we hang out."

"I don't eat lunch."

"Why not? It's free. Just go down and grab something or I can have someone get it for you."

"No, that food is nasty. I'm not eating that shit."

"Don't you bring anything to school then? Even a snack or something?"

"No, I just wait till I go home. I don't need anything."

"Bro, aren't you hungry?"

That was the end of the conversation. For the rest of that first day, Joe didn't answer any more questions. We just sat together in silence.

On Tuesday, as my wife was making my brown-bagged lunch, I asked her to make one for Joe as well, and she did. She wrote Joe's name on the front with a red heart around it. When Joe walked into his lunch detention that day, I handed him the bag, and we ate lunch together.

Joe didn't talk much that week, but again, it wasn't about the talking, it was about the act of care that took place. I wanted Joe to know that he was important enough to sit with, important enough to bring lunch to. I asked Joe a lot of questions that week, and finally by

Friday he answered a few and asked me a few as well. Toward the end of our time on Friday, Joe asked me if he could tell me something.

"Of course. Anything."

Joe went on to explain that, a few weeks before school started that year, he had been sitting with a good friend on the front steps of his friend's house. After realizing it was time to go, Joe hopped on his bike and began to ride home. When he was a few blocks away, he realized he had forgotten something and rode back to his friend's house. When he pulled up, he found his friend shot dead on the front steps of his house.

We just sat there in silence for what felt like forever.

"That could have been me," he said with his head hung low.

I didn't know what exactly to say. I grew up in Haddon Heights, New Jersey, in a house that never had its doors locked. What did I know about how to deal with an experience like this? They don't teach you this stuff in college or professional development. Part of me understands why. These moments are messy, and it's impossible to teach students in a college classroom how to deal with every conceivable situation. It's a matter of the heart, and matters of the heart can only be learned face to face. After a moment, I simply said, "I'm really sorry that happened, Joe. I'm honored that you would share your story with me, and I'm glad you're still here."

That was four years ago. Since then, Joe has eaten lunch with the rest of the misfits in my room every day. Even when I'm not there, he asks my neighbor, Ms. Flounders, to let him into my room so he doesn't have to eat in the lunchroom. On those days, he just sits quietly at my desk and keeps an eye on things for me. He is one of my favorite students who has ever walked into my classroom. He comes to me when he's having trouble inside or outside of the classroom, and he makes it a point to look out for others as well. His dream is to become an emergency room nurse or a paramedic. He wants to help people like his friend who lost his life on the front steps of his own home. It's important to point out here that, as teachers, we cannot fix children. We can sit with them. We can show genuine interest. And we can listen without feeling the need to have an answer, let alone the right answer. In doing so, we can form bonds that will exist indefinitely.

Your attention is far more important than your advice. No matter where you teach, you will encounter students who are in need of care. Sometimes you will feel prepared to help, and other times you will be caught off guard by a kid who walks in during your prep crying their eyes out. In those moments when you don't know what else to do, just listen. Many times, nothing you can say will make things better, but sitting with that student and listening will show that child that they are not alone. Sit in the muck with them, and you will have given that kid exactly what they needed: kinship. One of my heroes, Father Gregory Boyle, put it best in his book, *Tattoos on the Heart*: "You stand with the least likely to succeed until success is succeeded by something more valuable: kinship. You stand with the belligerent, the surly, and the badly behaved until bad behavior is recognized for the language it is: the vocabulary of the deeply wounded and of those whose burdens are more than they can bear."

In another example, one morning at my school we were told that someone had broken into the trailers. The invader destroyed walls and desks, threw paint and art supplies all over the art room, and smashed windows and teacher's personal belongings. As I walked to my classroom, I was anxious to say the least. I put a lot of time and effort into my classroom. From the decorations I'd bought or made myself to the *Romeo and Juliet* set my students had built, it was a huge commitment in time, effort, and money, and to think that someone had heartlessly entered our sacred space and destroyed what we had created was heartbreaking.

But as I walked up to the door of my classroom and unlocked the door, I discovered that not one thing had been touched or tampered with. My classroom was just the way I had left it the night before. I walked to the office to report what I had found. It felt like a miracle.

The classrooms on both sides of mine had been destroyed. Only my classroom and Mr. Manskopf's science lab had been untouched. Had the thief run out of time? Did the cops get there just before they had a chance to break my doors and windows in?

We were told that the police had caught the assailant; it turned out to be a student from our school, a young man who had been in trouble again and again. As retaliation, he broke into the school to get even and share his pain. When we don't teach young people what to do with their pain, we leave it up to them to figure it out. Mister Rogers had a song that I loved as a child. The lyrics went:

> What do you do with the mad that you feel
> When you feel so mad you could bite?
> When the whole wide world seems oh, so wrong…
> And nothing you do seems very right?
> What do you do? Do you punch a bag?
> Do you pound some clay or some dough?
> Do you round up friends for a game of tag?
> Or see how fast you go?
> It's great to be able to stop
> When you've planned a thing that's wrong,
> And be able to do something else instead
> And think this song:
> I can stop when I want to
> Can stop when I wish
> I can stop, stop, stop any time.
> And what a good feeling to feel like this
> And know that the feeling is really mine.
> Know that there's something deep inside
> That helps us become what we can.
> For a girl can be someday a woman
> And a boy can be someday a man.

As a high school teacher, I wouldn't necessarily read or sing this to my students, but the basic message here is crucial. We need to help our young people learn to deal with their anger, disappointment, heartache, and hatred. As a new teacher, this was a terrifying concept to me. How was I supposed to listen and give advice to kids who had grown up in an environment so different from the one I had? The answer comes from the point I made earlier, your *attention* is more important than your *advice*.

Giving students a safe space to talk about their feelings is more powerful than you can imagine, just as letting air out of an overinflated balloon prevents it from popping. That night I got a phone call from a student I had taught the year before, Romina. She had heard her friend had been arrested for breaking into the school and had gone to visit him. As they talked about what had happened, she asked him why he hadn't broken into Mr. Manskopf's or my room. His answer was simply, "I would never have done that. Those guys were always real cool with me." I didn't know what to do with that at first. It was too simple of an explanation.

I rarely tell this story, but I've thought about this incident a lot over the years. I have not gotten along with every student. Sometimes that has been because I didn't have the ability to break through or connect with a kid, and other times it's been because my attention wasn't wanted. On this occasion, I was able to get along with a student who didn't get along with most teachers. My failure was in not seeing what was happening with him and trying to help him address his feelings. I wish I had done more. Since then, I've tried to connect with every student. I am no savior. I am a member of a community of educators, and these days I act as such. I reach out to other teachers, and we work as a team to connect with students and families. Our goal is to meet whatever needs a student has. I don't know that any teacher can reach every student. When a team of caring individuals comes together and works together with the families, however, anything is possible.

Remember Student Two

One of my heroes, Rafe Esquith, was kind enough to be a guest one Sunday night on my live YouTube show, *Sunday Night Teacher Talk*. He broke down how he looks at students in his classroom. Rafe identifies three kinds of students. Student One is the kid everyone wants to teach because they show up ready to learn, eagerly volunteer to answer questions, excel at their work, and are a joy to be around. They love you and think your class is the best. They think critically and care about what's happening in class. Student Three is the student who requires the most attention. Whether it's behavior issues or just a general cry for help, Student Three requires a lot of attention and will take all they can get, any way they can get it. They are out loud with their behavior—touching other students, getting in fights, needing to have the last words, being rambunctious. They constantly require redirection and reinforcement and are like little fires you have to put out every few minutes.

Student Two, however, is almost invisible. They sit attentively in their seat every day and never raise their hands or seek attention in any way. They do their work quietly and never cause any trouble. These are the kids whose names we forget by the next year because they flew under the radar. Teachers can almost feel awkward interacting with them because they don't seem to want to talk. Especially in my beginning years as a teacher, I often overlooked these students. Type one and type three students make you feel like you are doing the good work you came to do in the classroom. Type one kids make you feel like a great teacher because they soak up everything you're pouring out. Type threes, like Joe, can make you feel like a superstar when you finally have the opportunity to celebrate hard-earned wins with them.

But type two students are usually the silent sufferers. They're the kids who either barely scrape by or fail the test by one or two questions, but you didn't even know they were struggling because they were so well-behaved and at least looked like they knew what was happening in class. It's crucial to care for these students. They're the kids who fall through the cracks and end up in my ninth-grade literature class still reading on a second-grade level. In my experience as a teacher, these are the kids who sometimes end up hurting themselves and others when their needs go unmet. In our classroom, my students and I make it a point not only to identify but to celebrate and care for the otherwise invisible kids, kids like my man Business Casual.

Business Casual is a skinny little dude. He is curiously happy for a high school kid and is a bundle of smiles and energy. He always says hi to everyone and tries to insert himself into conversations as a way to be a part of things. He can be too much for some people because he's still figuring out when enough is enough. His inability to chill has gotten him in trouble at times, getting him yelled at or punched in the eye. He's my favorite type of student because he is unapologetically himself. I met Business Casual his freshman year when he would visit the school store my students and I made to help us raise money for our first trip abroad. He was getting ready for wrestling practice, and he realized he didn't have wrestling shoes. This is a common issue with our wrestlers. When money is tight, our students often have to go without until we can figure out how to get them what they need. In this case, instead of wearing socks or sneakers, my man wore sweatpants and a T-shirt with his dress shoes. This is how he got his nickname: sweatpants + dress shoes = Business Casual.

One day during lunch I was walking the hallways, and I saw that Business Casual was just meandering around. I asked him what he was up to and why he wasn't in class. He told me he had lunch that period but he didn't like sitting in the lunchroom. I let him know that he was more than welcome to come and eat lunch in my room with the rest of the guys, and he was a little stunned. As it turns out, Business Casual had trouble making friends and felt lonely as a freshman at our school. Like a lot of his peers, Business Casual came from a surrounding neighborhood school, and when middle school was finished, he was sent by his grandmother to our school. A lot of parents and grandparents send their kids to our school because it's a safe alternative to some of the neighborhood schools in Philadelphia. This meant that Business Casual, like other kids in his situation, started the year alone. In retrospect, I think Business Casual reminded me a lot of myself when I was in high school. Starting off at a new school without any of your old friends and not having a place to belong is tough.

That afternoon, Business Casual came to my room, and he never left. Not only did he join us for lunch, but he also began coming into my room in the morning to say hi and see how my evening was and then staying after school so late sometimes that I would have to make him leave so I could go home. In my room, he made friends. Guys like Ham, David, and DJ Dirty Kev allowed Business Casual to be himself. They are a group within the group. They are, as ex-Navy SEAL and ultra-marathon runner David Goggins would say, "uncommon amongst uncommon men." They laugh and smile and talk about whatever they're interested in without ever trying to be cool. They do weird things like play "ping-pong" by placing blue painter's tape in the middle of a long table in the back of my room and hitting a stress ball back and forth with their hands. They have a "podcast" that's really just them standing around my plastic micro-phone bubble wand and talking about music, video games, and celebrities. It's the kind of thing that makes other faculty members stop in their tracks when they come into my room and wonder what in the world is going on.

I once met a teacher who explained to me how her school han-dled these type two students, and it was brilliant. About a month into the school year, the grade-level chairperson would project the name of every ninth-grade student onto the wall. She would then hand each teacher in the room a set of stickers in a different color. The teachers would then put a sticker next to the names of the students they felt they had a connection with. At the end of the activity, the teachers would see clearly which students were being cared for and which students needed attention. The next part of the meeting was used to divvy up the remaining students among the teachers. The teachers would take their new list of students and make sure they said hello or talked to all of them. It was a great way to make the invisible students feel visible. Not all relationships need to be deep. Simply acknowledging a student by saying "Hello," "Goodbye," or "I'm glad to see you" can be more than that kid is getting anywhere else. It also might be all that student wants. Your introverted students might be put off if you try to talk to them more than that, but a simple greeting or act of recognition can make all the difference.

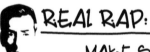 ## REAL RAP:

MAKE SURE EVERYONE IS SEEN

Whether it's your classroom, office, weight room, or lunchroom, having a safe space where students can gather—a place where teachers and students alike know that all are welcome and everyone is seen—is a beautiful gift to your school community. In these places, it is known that we take care of each other.

Every year a class of kids graduates and new kids join the fold. The community is an ever-evolving party of kindred spirits. Student relationships do not have to be over-complicated. My room is always full, but always chill. I set the tone, but as the students become more comfortable, they begin to take ownership of our time together. I rarely have to address behavior in my classroom before school, during lunch, or after the school day because the students address it for me. It is our classroom, and we take care of it together.

4.

TEACH THROUGH A LENS THE KIDS CARE ABOUT

An Epiphany

The principal pulled me aside one day and said that the school was looking to increase the number of electives being offered, and he asked if I would take on one of them. I was told I could teach anything I wanted so long as I could make the case that it was academic.

At first, I thought about what I would have liked when I was in high school. Then, I started to think of what cool stuff I was interested in now. Finally, it dawned on me that this is where I'd seen too many teachers go wrong before. I'd seen a lot of well-meaning teachers over the years create lessons and classes around the things they liked. The idea was a seemingly solid one. Teach something you love, and then let the passion you feel for that topic flow through you and fill your students with the same fire. However, time and again I saw teachers teach through their music, their movies, their interests, and their life views and not be able to excite the students, even though they themselves were bursting with excitement.

Those of us in education talk to students a lot about things like hard work and growth mindset. It's common to hear kids getting schooled on thinking outside of the box or trying something new. Ironically, all of this talk happens in schools that are plagued with worksheets and boring lesson plans. The same teachers that preach out-of-the-box thinking are handing out Xeroxed sheets from 1984. The classrooms where out-of-the-box thinking is demanded still have plain white walls and rows of desks and don't allow the kids any input about what and how they are going to learn.

The year before my elective began, another teacher in my school, RJ, created a class around the history and design of video games. Through the lens of video games, something both he and the students were passionate about, he was able to teach the kids about math and coding while also talking about the history of PAC-MAN and Halo. He taught it in my classroom, and it was fascinating. Each day I would try to get work done at my desk in the back of the room, and each day I would get drawn into the class. Often, I would go home and watch the end of a documentary or look further into an idea that RJ had brought up.

The funny thing about epiphanies is that they can reveal the same secrets again and again. They're like gifts that you need to be ready to accept. I knew that students learn much better when the content is relevant and relatable to their lives, but after sitting in that class and not only watching kids get excited about what they were learning but finding myself getting wrapped up too, the epiphany dawned on me. Teach the kids what you need them to learn through a lens that they are *already* interested in. BAM! How could I have missed this? I'd done it on a smaller scale for years but had never thought of teaching an entire class in that way. To make this happen, I needed to pay attention to what was going on at school. What movies are the kids going to see? What music are they listening to? What shows have their attention?

In my fifth year in the classroom, I noticed that all of my students were watching the show *Jersey Shore* on MTV. Every Monday they would come into homeroom literally yelling and screaming about what had happened the night before. "Snooki is a ho! I can't believe she was twerking like that in the club!" "Ronnie is dumb as hell! He keeps taking Sam back, and she don't even like him like that. That sucker is getting played!" I had no idea what everyone was talking about, but I did know that everyone's vocabulary grades sucked. Every Monday when I tried to give them that week's vocabulary words the kids were more caught up in what The Situation (one of the show's main characters) was doing than they were in my lesson. One Sunday I decided to watch an episode and see what everyone was yelling about. It was literally one of the dumbest shows I'd ever seen. I couldn't figure out why anyone would watch it. No one on the show was very good at anything. They didn't say anything particularly interesting. It was like watching the drunks that use the pay phone in front of my house. It was loud and obnoxious, but it was what my students cared about.

That night I changed all of my vocabulary slides. Instead of having the wolf in sheep's clothing as my picture for the word "furtive," I had a picture of Sammy in the club as she was looking to hook up. In lieu of the picture of the storm clouds I had for the word "looming," I had a picture of Pauly D heading up the stairs to the rooftop deck at the shore house where he was about to get into it with one of his housemates. When I tell you this changed how my students interacted with my vocabulary lessons, I mean it changed everything. Kids were suddenly drawn to the images. It helped them remember the words and their definitions and, as a bonus, it gave us a chance to compare and contrast the reading we were doing in class with the show.

That year I had begun successfully integrating what the students were interested in into my lessons. Now I had the opportunity to create an entire class that would allow me to teach important content through a lens that the kids were already passionate about. This challenge made me reflect on what my students cared and talked about. Certainly a lot of them were outliers—kids who liked Pokémon and Magic cards, anime, hardcore music, YouTube, poetry, and comic books. The majority of my students, though, talked about four things: girls, sports, video games, and hip-hop. RJ was already teaching video games. As a person who spent way too much time in right field as a kid, I had never cared or learned much about sports. And I wasn't going to teach a class about girls. Hip-hop, however, was a possibility.

The problem was that I was the old dude who listened to old dude hip-hop. I didn't know anything about what kids were listening to now. I grew up in an all-white, middle-class neighborhood that looked like a scene out of *Pleasantville* or *The Sandlot*.

When I was twelve years old, my cousin Jason, who lived in the Olney section of Philly, introduced me to hip-hop. At that age, the socially conscious lyrics of Public Enemy and NWA and the power of the stories and ideas these artists were conveying were lost on me. However, something about the beats, the vibe, and the wordplay pulled me in. I was immediately drawn to the vibes of artists like Boogie Down Productions, The Beastie Boys, Tribe Called Quest, and Digable Planets, and I still listen to them to this day. Like many of us, I felt a connection to the music I grew up with but lost interest in what was new and fresh in the genre.

I was also intrigued to find that many of my students didn't seem to have a sense of the history of the art form they loved so much. Whereas in rock, country, and jazz, many young fans are interested in earlier performers and how the music has changed over time, my students who loved hip-hop did not seem to have the same interest. The focus in hip-hop was on what was fresh and new. Growing up as a drummer, I loved finding out who my idols looked up to. If I found out that Stewart Copeland of The Police or Dave Abbruzzese of Pearl Jam got their inspiration from Ginger Baker, I immediately went out and bought a Cream album. On the other hand, my students wouldn't hear Eminem or Meek Mill say that Nas or Treach from Naughty by Nature were their all-time favorite rappers and then go listen to their music. I don't say this as a diss either. I love the idea of always looking forward and of focusing on innovation as opposed to looking back. I'm just noting that young hip-hop fans are different in this way.

My decision was cemented by the fact that this seemed to be total white space for me as a teacher. No one else that I knew or that I could find online was doing this, so I could create something original that my students wouldn't be able to find elsewhere.

The next step was to come up with a curriculum. I decided to base the class, which I named the History of Hip-Hop, on the four main tenets of hip-hop: emceeing, deejaying, break dancing, and graffiti art. I would dive deep into the history of each branch and connect it with information that I wanted or needed my students to know. This was not a subject I knew a lot about. I knew some stuff, but I also know some stuff about cooking, and no one should ask me how to do it. This was perfect because it would allow me to model for my students what it was like to learn something, and not just on a surface level so I could skate by. I had to learn about the history of the music and the culture on a deep enough level to help my students better understand what they were experiencing and where it all started.

As I was building the class curriculum, I would regularly tell my classes what I had learned or uncovered. Every time I got a new shipment of books in the mail, I would do an unboxing with the students and tell them about the books I had picked, like *The Rap Year Book* by Shea Serrano, *The Hip-Hop Wars* by Tricia Rose, and *Can't Stop Won't Stop* by Jeff Chang, and why I picked them. I would find out from my students which artists I should be listening to and why. Then I would listen to every artist and come back to my students with follow-up questions. We would talk about parts of songs we liked, references made by the artist that we needed to investigate, or samples that we heard in the songs that we knew from other albums. The more I learned, the more I shared. It ended up being an experiment in showing the students just what active learning looked like.

That summer I did a deep dive into the world of hip-hop music and culture. Starting from African drums and dance and then moving west to Jamaica and what became known as the Jamaican sound system, then north to 1520 Sedgwick Avenue in the Bronx where Kool Herc would deejay parties in his apartment building. From there, this new music would spread to the rest of the five boroughs and out to the world. I learned that graffiti art started in my city of Philadelphia. I studied the fashion and its evolution, the DJs, cyphering's roots in the slave trade, and the way the art of rap changed over time.

It was an immersion for me, for sure, but it was fun to learn so much about a topic I knew my students would be interested in. That fall as school was about to start, I knew I wouldn't be able to grab the students' attention in a powerful way if I just stood in front of the room and spouted facts about hip-hop. I would have to *show* them hip-hop. I started reaching out to artists who were immersed in the art form and culture I had been studying. The best way I found to do this was by sending direct messages (DMs) on Instagram. As it turns out, this is *the* right medium to connect with someone. Nearly everyone I reached out to responded positively and was happy to speak with my students. I can't stress how important it has been to have guests come into our classroom or meet with us virtually through Skype or Google Hangouts. Let me break it down a little further.

What if you signed up for a cooking class and instead of cooking you listened to someone talk about cooking? What if you took a dance class, but instead of putting on your dancing shoes and getting sweaty on the dance floor, you watched a video or read a book together about the theory behind the steps and how to do them? It's just not the same. How could I expect my students to understand what the art of deejaying required without putting their hands on a turntable? How would they appreciate what it meant to be an MC if they didn't stand in front of a crowded classroom to spit the bars they had been crafting? How could you wrap your head around street art if you didn't see it up close and have an artist walk you through what it takes to create a tag or a mural? Furthermore, what would it be like if that same artist put a graffiti can in your hand so you could try it yourself?

I had zero dollars to pay anyone to honor us with their presence. Instead, they all volunteered out of the kindness of their hearts. Poets, rappers, DJs, drummers, and fashion designers all either came to our classroom or had us come to them for free. Why would they do that? I asked every single one of them, and they all had the same answer: "I wish this class had existed when I was in high school." I had created a class that the guests themselves wanted to be a part of. In turn, these guests enriched the students' learning experiences in ways I never could have.

The History of Hip-Hop was one of the best things I ever did in my classroom. It created a space for my students and me to talk about what it means to be a man, the power of your story, the school-to-prison pipeline, the almost nonexistent presence of the LGBTQ community in the rap scene, how Snoop and Shakespeare are more alike than my students realize, entrepreneurship, Black Lives Matter, poetry, art, slavery, and a host of other topics. After talking about these topics, the students created projects, wrote poems and rhymes, created tags, and connected what we learned in our literature class with what we did in the hip-hop class. We had cyphers every Friday where the kids would have rap battles over beats made by their friends to see who had the wordplay that would most move the room.

One particular Friday, our class was on a roll. One of my students, whom we called Talky Talk because he never stopped talking, brought in his turntables and speakers and shared his skills. While he was mixing and with the base hitting so hard the walls shook, my class took turns performing in front of the class. At that point, one of my former students, Daseim Henry, walked through the door. Daseim was a quiet, humble senior at our school, not so much shy as laid-back. He was the kind of guy who was known among those he wanted to know him. That Friday though, my man blasted through my door with a hall pass in his hand, and without a heads-up or an introduction, he grabbed the mic and tore into a song he had written. His gravelly voice filled the room, and his words blew the roof off. His conviction and rhymes literally made the class freeze in place. The moment he finished, he put the mic down, turned toward the exit, and walked right out the door before any of us had a chance to make heads or tails of what had just happened. As the door closed behind him and the kids sat in disbelief, one of my students looked back at me and said, "Reynolds! Who the fuck was that bull?" The classroom erupted in laughter and cheers.

I later pulled Daseim aside and asked him what in the world had happened. He said he had been writing songs for years under the stage name Mad Squablz. He had heard what was happening in our classroom on Friday afternoons, which wasn't a surprise since I'd had to warn my neighbors about the bass that was certainly penetrating the walls, so he asked his teacher if he could have a hall pass to go see me. He then came in and decimated the scene. The next trimester, Daseim signed up for my elective. It gave kids like him, kids who otherwise often go unnoticed, a chance to share their gift in school. Just as RJ's video game class had given gamers a chance to dive deep into the inner workings of the digital world they loved, my class gave artists and poets a chance to share their story.

It is not my intention in writing this to have every teacher start teaching the History of Hip-Hop. Maybe your students don't like that type of music, or perhaps your school wouldn't hear of such a class. My intention is to get you thinking about what your students *do* like. What would your students lose their minds over? What would make them want to come to school? What class would make them sorry they were absent or late? Maybe a class based on anime or comic books? Skateboarding? Entrepreneurship? Social media? Breakfast cereal? Action figures? Lego? YouTube? If you don't know what your students are into, just ask them! Can you imagine if your teacher had walked into your class when you were in school and asked you what you wanted to learn about? It would have blown your mind! Much of our required curriculum can be taught through the lens of topics our students are actually interested in. Take a chance, and just do it!

Connecting Pop Culture with School Culture

How do you get started doing this in your own class? Here are a few simple ways I've been able to connect my students' interests with my English curriculum.

Every year when I tell my students we are going to read *The Merchant of Venice* or *Romeo and Juliet*, they let out a collective moan. They hate it. "Reynolds, why do we have to read this? It's so boring! We don't even know what he's talking about!" It's the same complaint every year. The thing is, it's absolutely not boring. To prove how un-boring Shakespeare is, I often tell my students the basic plotline of *Titus Andronicus*, and every time they freak out. Cutting out people's tongues and turning your enemies into meat pies for their mothers to eat sounds more like *Game of Thrones* than Shakespeare. As for the language, I just explain how much fun language can be and how slang is always changing. When you're young, it's a point of pride to know a term or phrase that others, especially older folks, don't know. Since my second year of teaching, I have kept a journal of all of the words I think are the best—slang terms and phrases that my students love and I think are particularly funny or witty or poetic. Every year before we do Shakespeare, I pull out that notebook, and I share with them a list of what I've heard over the year. Jawn, hop in the bub, edges going naked, chippin', drawin', bangin', in the cut, molly whopped . . . The list goes on. I find it funny that each year my students don't know what 90 percent of those terms mean because hip-hop stops for no one. As I said before, the focus is on what's fresh and new. We then take a look at Snoop. I typically use the lyrics from Snoop's song *Drop It Like It's Hot* because it's a song everyone knows and, for some reason, it has stuck around. I ask the students to circle all of the words that their grandmother or great-grandmother would not know or at least wouldn't understand in the same way. Then I ask them to replace the circled words with terms their family would know. When Snoop uses words like "crib" and "pigs," the students need to identify and replace them with vocabulary their grandma would understand. If we read this song literally, it sounds like a man who arranges dates with prostitutes is sleeping in a baby's bed and that Snoop's advice to those listening would be to park your vehicle post haste if you are being chased by swine.

When Shakespeare writes "If love be rough with you, be rough with love. Prick love for pricking and you beat love down" or "Death, that hath suck'd the honey of thy breath hath had no power yet upon thy beauty," we know that he is saying something beyond the literal meanings of the words, just as Snoop was doing. This lesson is a reminder to students that language can be fun, and although Shakespeare is often seen as the holy grail of literature, he was indeed playing with language in a way that excited his audience—the same thing every hip-hop artist has done since the beginning of the art.

Countless novels and films recount stories of people crash-landing in a remote place and having to survive—*Cast Away, Lost, The 100, The Edge, Alive, Robinson Crusoe, Swiss Family Robinson.* I use these familiar stories to help me teach William Golding's *Lord of the*

Flies. When I want to create a connection point or stir up interest in my students, I just look where they are looking and build the bridge. It's easy to disregard the references to pop culture that kids make on a daily basis, but when we dial into what they are talking about, we begin to see patterns form. If a number of students mention a particular movie, video game, music artist, or television show to me, I make it a point to check it out. I then try to use those student interests in what I'm teaching. When *Lost* was the number one show on television and all of my students were locked into the final season, I made sure to connect it to *Lord of the Flies.* Both *Lord of the Flies* and *Lost* began with a plane crash and with the survivors having to figure out how to survive and govern themselves. When *Lost* ended and my new students began watching the CW show *The 100,* a drama about a group of teenagers that crash-land on Earth after living in space their entire lives, I shifted the lesson and began making the same connections with *The 100* as I had done with *Lost.*

What does this actually look like in the classroom from day to day? I start teaching *Lord of the Flies* by projecting a still image of the jungle onto the board in the front of the classroom. I also play jungle sounds over the speakers in our classroom to set the mood and peak the students' interest. When the students come in, I tell them to sit anywhere they'd like but to make sure their eyes are closed or their heads are down. We take thirty seconds or so and settle into the sounds of the jungle. I then read a passage about what it might feel like to crash-land on an island. I want to create an image for them of how hot it is and how bright the sun is. I also ask questions about what they would do first if they were lost on a deserted island. Who would be in charge? What would be their part in the community of survivors? When I finish reading, I have them sit up and answer two writing prompts. One: What would you do first to ensure your survival? And two: How would it feel to have no adults on the island? After they write and we discuss their answers, I show them the opening scene from *Lost* or *Castaway.* These scenes provide a great way to create a visual of what it might be like to be in Ralph's and Jack's shoes. We then write and discuss what new aspects of being stranded—things the students hadn't considered before—the scenes brought to their minds.

As we read the book, I continue to pull in other engaging clips from movies and television shows to keep the students interested in and focused on what the novel is describing. When one of the main characters, Piggy, is continually bullied by other boys on the island, we connect it to how Peter Parker was bullied in the beginning of *Spiderman* or how some of my students might have dealt with bullying in the past. The idea is to take what students might initially think is an outdated and out-of-touch text and breathe new life into it by showing that the human experience isn't so different from story to story and, indeed, among their own lives.

Homer's *The Odyssey* is one of the oldest stories to chronicle the hero's journey, but that makes it fun because it can be connected to just about any movie about heroes—*The Avengers, Star Wars, Harry Potter, Hunger Games,* and so on. When students see that this dusty old tale is the blueprint for some of their favorite shows and movies, they are not only drawn in, but they also have a reference point to connect what they are learning with what they already know.

As an opening activity for *The Odyssey*, the students learn about Joseph Campbell's theory of the hero's journey. I then give the students a blueprint of the hero's journey and have them connect it to their favorite hero movie or show. This does not need to be a superhero. It can be anyone from Rocky to a character from their favorite video game. After the students complete their rough drafts, we work on creating posters for each of their heroes' journeys. The posters are displayed around the room and are referenced as we work our way through the book. When Odysseus enters his "inmost cave," we talk about the dark night of the soul that every hero must travel through to become the best version of themselves.

When we read *The Odyssey,* we also draw comparisons between Odysseus's wife, Penelope, and strong female characters like Sansa Stark and Princess Leia. We discuss what characteristics these women had that set them apart from the stereotypes thrust upon them by their in-story environments. To make the text even more relevant to the students, we then write about and discuss examples of strong female role models in their own lives. In doing this, the character of Queen Penelope evolves from a mere queen who was seemingly abandoned by her husband to a woman my students can view with the same kind of respect they have for the important women in their lives.

When we read *Fahrenheit 451* by Ray Bradbury, we discuss how much Bradbury's vision of the dystopian future actually came true. When Mildred wants to escape her dull, depressing life, she puts "sea shells" in her ears; it's not a far cry from how my students constantly walk around with Airpods in their ears. Mildred also loves to be a part of an alternative reality when she watches television on the "parlor walls." In the book, Bradbury predicted that televisions would one day be as large as the walls in our homes. If we take this a step further, we can connect the idea with movies like *The Matrix* or the novel *Ready Player One.* Montag, like Neo, needs to decide whether he wants to know the truth about the world he is living in. Similarly, Wade Watts, the protagonist of *Ready Player One,* feels more connected to his virtual friends than he does with anyone he knows in the physical world.

By making these connections, the students begin to see that the themes and ideas in the texts we read as a class are the same that run through their favorite media and, in fact, through their own lives. How many of our students try to escape reality through social media, music, or video games? How many of them have friends online whom they have never met face to face but whom they feel more connected to than the people they interact with in their own physical worlds? Literature often acts as a mirror that reflects back to us who we really are. It can also act as a bridge to help us get to the next level in our lives. Part of the excitement of being a reader is learning more about ourselves and the world around us.

These are just a few of the ideas I use in class. The list is ever evolving because the students' interests are always changing. What worked for you this year might not work for you next year. Every once in a while, if you dare to go full throttle, you will find lessons that bring the whole class together to make something truly magical.

The Romeo and Juliet Project

In my third year of teaching, my classroom was in a trailer behind the school. The entire ninth-grade team relocated in an effort by the administration to keep the young freshmen from the influence of the upperclassmen. Although I wasn't behind this idea of exclusion, I embraced my new space. It was the first time in three years that I had windows in my classroom. For the previous two years, I would often show up at work at six in the morning and leave around six or seven in the evening, which meant I came into my windowless classroom before the sun came up and then left after the sun went down. I was so pale I looked like one of those vampires from *Twilight*.

Even though the trailer leaked, parts of the floor were too soft and rotten to walk on, there was no hallway, and to get your copies or use the bathroom you occasionally had to walk through rain or snow, the trailer was a pretty sweet deal. For one thing, no one ever came out to see what we were doing. It was like moving into your parents' basement or garage. As long as you didn't make too much noise, everyone forgot you existed. This worked fine for me because I wanted to try some crazy stuff that year, and it was easier knowing that no one was watching. It also meant I could come and go as I pleased. Our school didn't allow teachers to be in the building without a supervisor present. I could be in my trailer any time I wanted, however, because I had a key.

A lot of memorable moments occurred in the two years that I was in my double-wide. Two, however, stand out as literally changing the way I approached class and relationships with students. The first one happened just after we started our *Romeo and Juliet* unit. The year before, my students and I had transformed our classroom into the Globe Theatre. None of us had any experience in building a set for a play, but we figured it out together. When we were finished, our classroom was a cardboard version of the famous Globe Theatre. We then read *Romeo and Juliet* and acted it out as we went. This year I wanted to build off of that idea and take our set production and reading of the play to the next level. Before we even started, people in the school were excited about the project because the students I'd had the previous year had told the freshmen what we had done.

Your reputation will do more for your classroom management and student engagement than you can anticipate. If word gets around that you are strict, fun, funny, a hard-ass, or a pushover, your reputation will precede you. In the case of our Shakespeare unit, word had gotten around that this was going to be big. When I told the students the time had come, you could feel the energy in the room. I said to my class, "For this unit, I want you to go big. I encourage you to think outside of the box. Go nuts! If you can't figure out how to make your ideas work, then come to me and I'll help you make them happen." That weekend I went back to Home Depot and again drove away with as many cardboard boxes as I could fit into my good old Ford Escort. I shoved them in the trunk and the backseat. They sat shotgun, and I tied them to the roof. On Monday, we got started. We made an actual balcony complete with a tree for Romeo to hide behind, swords, clouds, stars, a crypt, a shelter where Romeo could hide out when he was in exile, and a box office to sell tickets at. It was legit! Then, on the second day of building, my phone rang.

"Mr. Reynolds?"

"Yes, this is he."

"Did you order a lumber delivery?"

"What? A lumber delivery? No. Why would I do that?"

"A man is in the front office saying he has a lumber delivery for your class."

What in the world was this? Why would someone have a lumber delivery for me? I didn't have a budget. I had just driven to the school with a ridiculous, cartoon-worthy amount of cardboard stuffed into my car because I couldn't afford five cents worth of supplies. Just then the principal walked into my classroom like Kramer into Seinfeld's apartment. "Mr. Reynolds! What's the deal with this lumber?!" He was clearly perplexed, with the look of someone who couldn't answer for what his employee had been up to.

After I explained that I hadn't made the order, the principal looked around at the thirty or so students who were painting, hot gluing, and designing our set. His look did not seem supportive. It looked more like, "What on earth is this clown doing? Isn't this English class? Shouldn't they be reading and stuff?" I could see that I needed to go to the office and find out what was going on. I told the class I'd be right back.

"Reynolds, where you going?" one of my students asked.

"I need to run to the office. They said there's a delivery for me, and I need to see what's up."

"Oh! Is it the wood we ordered?"

"What? Huh? You ordered lumber?"

"Yeah, my group all chipped in and ordered wood so we could build a stage. You said to think outside of the box."

He was right; I did say that. I told the principal that the order was indeed for my class. The boys walked out with me and unloaded the plywood and two-by-fours that had been delivered. My room looked like something on *Hoarders*. There was so much stuff in it that you could barely move. But the boys who ordered the lumber were determined to build a stage to perform on, so for the next week they stayed after school with me and learned how to do it.

None of them knew the first thing about using tools, so the week was a bit of a how-to workshop in carpentry and stage design. By the end of the week, however, we had constructed an eight-by-ten-foot stage complete with pillars and a canvas drop-cloth ceiling. To mimic the Globe Theatre, the students decorated the ceiling with astrological signs, and the whole thing was lit with cheap aluminum clamp-on lights from Mr. Manskopf's science room. We had enough wood left over to build two caskets that we housed in our "crypt." My trailer had a pretty big area that was supposed to be a bathroom, but instead of outfitting it with actual bathroom stuff, it was left empty and looked like a large closet with a toilet hole in the ground. This became our crypt. It was an excellent addition to our set.

The class was equally as incredible as the room was. The kids came in to work on their projects during every extra moment they had. They were everything you would want to see in a class— engaged, working together, problem solving, excited for themselves and others, and learning, truly learning.

During all of the projects I've ever done that were way over the top, certain students have really come alive. The *Romeo and Juliet* project happened years ago, but I still keep up with a number of those students to this day—kids like Colleen Sanchez, Genesis Hernandez, Donovan Smalls, and Christian Fernandez. It's amazing to see these young men and women still getting after it. Teaching them back then was like getting a glimpse of who they would become.

 ## REAL RAP:

THIS IS HARD BUT WORTH IT

Seeing your students dig deep and make your classroom come alive is the most magical and gratifying thing you can do as a teacher. At the same time, it can be completely overwhelming. Thirty kids wielding glue guns, paint brushes, utility knives, power drills, and handsaws while jamming to loud music to get the vibe right can cause sensory overload. It's like being in a Home Depot that has been turned into a nightclub and filled with kittens wielding weapons of mass creation.

Not everyone in your school or district will be thrilled with your idea to go for it, either. In my case, I've had teachers tell the students I was wasting valuable time or not teaching the approved curriculum. In my first school, I had the administration make fun of me during board meetings for "playing" rather than teaching my students. I am not impervious to this sort of negativity. It hurts. A lot. But what's the alternative? To teach lessons in a manner that helps the administration or other faculty members feel better but bores me and, worse, my students into apathy?? No way. The best moments I've had in the classroom have been because I've had the courage to teach in ways that I wish I had been taught and that make kids want to come to class.

My dear teachers, I know what some schools try to get you to do. I know about their scripted lesson plans and classroom rules; their weak, cookie-cutter IEPs and 504 plans; their restrictions; their outdated reading lists; and their teach-to-the-test mentality. Your job is to do what is right for your students. Look for other teachers who are doing amazing things. These folks exist, and not just a few. There are *tons*. Look in your school, your district, or online. I run a closed Facebook group, Real Rap with Reynolds Teacher Talk, that grew out of my YouTube channel. It's filled with thousands of amazing teachers from all over the world who are teaching every conceivable subject and grade level. Like you, they are all trying to be the greatest teachers they can possibly be. You are not alone. Other educators around the world are looking for connections with people just like you. Find your crew.

There is no silver bullet in teaching. I know that social media and even this book might give you the impression that all the other teachers are winning while you struggle to get your kids to stay awake and pay attention, let alone show up early and stay late to create stunning projects. Let's be clear: I have had my share of kids who refuse to engage no matter what—kids who came to my hip-hop class and just sat in the corner because it was "boring"; kids who complained about building sets for Shakespeare and acting out the play and asked if instead they could just have a worksheet and be left alone. Real rap: you will rarely find an activity, project, book, guest, or idea that everyone likes. You need to be okay with that. It is not a reflection on you. Not every assignment is for every kid. Your job is to light the fireworks, not to make everyone enjoy them.

When you start that next lesson and the rest of the staff looks at you like you must have lost your mind, when the security officer walks into your room because the kids are shouting and cheering because their friends are giving it their all in a rap battle or poetry slam, when the administration wants to lock up the building but you and your students are staying late to create projects, science experiments, or stories that are next level, remember that you are not alone and that you are doing the most important work in the world. You're lighting the fuse of wonder and possibility in a child.

5
REAL-WORLD LEARNING

You Are the Average of the People You Hang Out With

Jim Rohn, an entrepreneur and motivational speaker, says, "You are the average of the five people you hang out with the most." I'll go deeper into this quote in a later chapter, but my point here is that the people you choose to be around will influence who you become.

West Philadelphia can be a rough place. While many of the families that our school serves are able to provide safe and loving environments for their children, others struggle to make ends meet. In many cases, our students turn to the streets because they can make money a lot faster and more easily selling drugs than working at the local fast-food restaurant. I've lost too many students over the years to gun violence. I've had former students end up in prison. I've had to hold kids up from leaving at the end of the day because of gun-shots down the street from the school. To many of our kids, the call of the streets is so consistent and alluring that it can feel impossible to reject.

Marie was a student who lived with her family in her grandma's basement. She slept with her parents and her sister in the same base-ment bedroom. Her mom worked two jobs, and her father hadn't worked for as long as she could remember. During her senior year, Marie wanted to get a job so she could go on the senior trip and pay for her prom dress. For a job at a fast-food joint, she would need black pants and shoes, so she asked her dad to front her the cash so she could get what she needed. Her pop told her that she would have to figure it out on her own. He had just stocked up on his weed supply and was out of money. While we ate lunch in my classroom the next day, Marie and I talked about how she could get the money. I knew full well that in the past Marie had worked on corners in Philly selling drugs to make ends meet. The allure was always there. You didn't need to get a uniform to work the corner. You didn't need to pay taxes. That day after lunch I went to an ATM and got out sixty dollars and gave it to Marie at the end of the school day. I had just done a speaking engagement and had some extra cash, though that's not always the case. She was overwhelmed with appreciation and excited about being able to make her own money at a job that was safe. Not long after Marie started her position, she and her step-brother were attending a candlelight vigil for a close friend who had been murdered. As they left, Marie went one way, and her step-brother went the other. On his way home, Marie's stepbrother was killed by a group of men for reasons Marie didn't know. We didn't see Marie in school for weeks after that horrific night. She had quit her job and stopped coming to school. She eventually came back to school and tried to fall back into her rhythm, but it was understand-ably all too much for her. Sometimes a student's hurt can only be healed by time and space. In such situations, all we can do is sit with them in their hurt. Sadly, Marie's family decided that moving away was the best idea for all of them. Her best friend, Jay, sat in my classroom all through the next day just to be sad in private. On top of all of this, Jay had to contend with his own troubles.

Jay's home was always an issue for him. His mom worked several jobs to support her family. His dad was in and out of the house but never had a job. Jay didn't like his mother going out at night by herself, so if she had an errand to run, he would always go with her. One evening, they both ran to the store to get ingredients for dinner. When they got to the checkout counter, Jay's mom placed the items on the counter and handed her debit card to the cashier. The cashier ran the card and then informed Jay's mother that her card had been denied. "Reynolds, the lady announced it so loud the whole store could hear her. It was embarrassing as shit. I just grabbed my mom's arm and walked out of the store," Jay said as he looked at the floor. "We just went home with no dinner. I told her she has two weeks to figure something out with my dad or I'm going to take care of it." By "take care of it," Jay meant he would go back to work for his cousin as a lookout for his hustle in North Philly.

"Bro," I said, "why don't you go and get a real job to help your mom out? I can help you fill out applications, and I can even drive you around to drop them off and go to interviews." I already knew what his response would be. It was the same response I'd heard from students plenty of times before. Jobs were few and far between. When you're young, many factors restrict when and how much you can work, and it wasn't always worth the time of taking the bus and the train to get to a job that paid minimum wage. The street pays cash, and it pays nightly.

What do you do when students need more than you can give? When homework doesn't get done because the power got shut off? When kids sleep all day in your class because they were removed from their homes by Child and Youth Services in the middle of the night? When kids can't pay attention because breakfast was a small bag of chips and a soda because mom had to get the water turned back on? When kids don't want to go home at the end of the day because their dad has been drinking again and they don't know what kind of madness they'll be walking into at home that night?

No matter where you teach, in the hood or in the finest private schools in the world, your students will have struggles that you are not prepared to deal with. Sometimes you can reach out to your guidance department or your administration for help. Sometimes you and your fellow teachers will be able to formulate a plan to help. Other times you will be stuck, and helping students find the value not only in your class but also in themselves can seem impossible.

What I've found to help the most is to keep it real with students. In an earlier chapter I talked about how you, the teacher, can keep it real in your classrooms and interactions with your students, but here I want to talk about sending up the Bat Signal for help. Sometimes you cannot be enough. Sometimes the school and the social work department, the parents, the school therapist, and the after-school program aimed at helping "troubled" students are also not enough. What can be enough is the real world. Author and life coach Tony Robbins once said, "[S]uccess leaves clues, and . . . people who produce outstanding results do specific things to create those results." What my students needed was to find connections with people who shared a common starting point with them but who had found a way to happiness and success. I needed to make those experiences happen. As teachers we are often not enough, but we have the power to reach out to those who might be.

Super-Secret Class Trips

Inspired by my absolute teacher hero, Rafe Esquith, I knew when I started teaching that I wanted to expose my students to as many experiences and opportunities inside as well as outside of the classroom as I could. Rafe is known for taking his students all over the world.

In his book, *There Are No Shortcuts,* Rafe says, "I've learned the best reason to take children on the road: children learn and understand how to behave by being exposed to new situations and watching others. . . . As a teacher of children from economically disadvantaged backgrounds, I came to understand that my students would work harder for a better life if they saw the life they were working for."

As a first-year teacher in one of the poorest neighborhoods in America, I yearned to do the same for my students. However, as any teacher who's been teaching for five minutes can tell you, it's next to impossible to find money for such endeavors. I thus made it a point to find free or super-cheap experiences for my kids. I called everywhere I could—theaters, businesses, restaurants, libraries. I hit up anyone who might be able to hook something up for us. For our first trip, we headed to the University of Pennsylvania to see a performance of *Romeo and Juliet.* None of my students had ever been to an Ivy League school, and most had never been to Philadelphia, even though Camden was directly across the river from Philly. The school had the maintenance man drive us fifteen minutes over the bridge to U Penn, and we walked into the theater to see the play. Everyone enjoyed it, even Mrs. Gonzalez, a parent chaperone who spoke almost no English. Years later, when I saw her again at her daughter's wedding, we laughed as she excitedly recounted our adventure.

After the play, we went to a beautiful lunch and music venue in University City called World Cafe Live. It was created in an old factory and is decorated in a fun art deco theme. The food costs quite a bit more than my students were used to, so I called ahead and asked if they could have one or two dishes for my students that were more affordable but still had that great vibe that came with the rest of the menu. The restaurant was happy to do it, and the students enjoyed eating food that looked like art more than it did food. It was an awesome experience. When we returned to school, the kids told everyone about the college campus and the architecture, the play and the scenery, and the food and the beautiful restaurant we went to. The students who were not able to go that time could not wait for their opportunity to come with us the next time.

Here are my rules for these class trips. First, everyone has to pay, even if it's only five dollars. Students who pay for a meal or an experience, even if it's just a fraction of the total cost, have a richer experience. When you are handed something for free, it's easy to discard it. I've had free opportunities come our way before, and students have backed out of them last minute because they didn't need to be committed. On the other hand, if a student pays even a tiny contribution toward their experience, they now own that trip, and if they choose not to go, they will lose out.

Next, not everyone goes on every trip. Taking class trips with an entire school or an entire grade level or even an entire class is enough to make your face melt off. I've been on a few class trips with my own children, the ones I made, and it is always wild and anxiety ridden. Trips with more manageable numbers, ten to twenty students, go way more smoothly, and they allow you to experience the adventure with each child.

Also, taking only a handful of kids allows you to take the right mix of students. My groups are usually a selection of kids who are hard workers and students who I think could use a special experience. Maybe the latter group has a difficult situation going on at home or they've been invisible to the rest of the school all year. In either case, class adventures allow you to shed some light on those who deserve it. This also lets you use class trips as an incentive for students who are not yet ready for these experiences. Students whose behavior or in-class performance does not warrant the privilege of a trip always have the opportunity to work toward going.

I also do not travel with those I do not trust. When I take my high school students out, I do not babysit them. I don't take anyone who's going to get themselves in trouble or make me or the school look bad. That doesn't mean I just pick all the well-behaved kids. It means that I discuss with them before they go what my expectations are. I explain that these trips are a privilege and that I want them to get everything out of it that they can. I make sure they know that they, as students, are important to me, and I am bringing them because I see something in them. Class trips can be the gasoline that we pour on kids' fires.

The play was the first of a small handful of official trips the school would allow me to take over the course of the next five years. I put trip request forms in for a ton of other trips, and all of them were denied. We didn't have the funds, or the bus was broken, or they couldn't get a substitute for my other classes, or the school didn't see the value in it. Our class was once invited by MTV to attend a special screening of a new documentary they had produced. The entire experience was free. All of the students would receive a free lunch and would be able to take part in a conversation after the film with some of its creators. The morning of the trip, my students and I were eagerly waiting outside of the school doors for our bus to pick us up when the principal came out and told us we all needed to go back to class. He told us he was canceling the trip because he didn't have enough teachers in the building that day. The kids were crushed. I had hand-picked students to go, and I had been talking up the trip for weeks. All of the kids had spent extra time learning about the topic of the documentary, so they would be able to engage fully and make the most of the experience. I hate letting kids down. It is one of those things in life that just destroys me. When I say we are going to do something, I want to follow through no matter what. I would never let such a thing happen again.

During my second year of teaching, I had one of my overall favorite classes of all time. I don't know how it happened, but I got a group of kids who were willing to go with whatever ridiculous idea I threw at them. Early that fall, I got word that one of my favorite poets, Derrick Brown, was traveling to Philadelphia with some poet friends to do a show. They had just finished filming some of their poetry in New York City as part of HBO's *Def Poetry Jam*. The show in Philly was the next night, and it was too short of a turnaround for me to inform parents and get permission slips to all the families, so I asked Derrick if he and his friends would be willing to stop into our classroom and do an impromptu show for our class. To my absolute surprise, he said yes!

The plan was to have them come in and do a quick set to whatever class was in my room at the time. This was going to be awesome! I don't know about your experience, but my kids don't get super excited about poetry. To be honest, until I read Derrick's writing, I thought poets just walked around in all black with berets on while smoking clove cigarettes. I still think the clove cigarette thing is true, but the writers who were a part of Derrick's publishing company, Write Bloody Publishing, wrote poetry for kids who don't like poetry. This was one of those moments you know your students will remember for the rest of their lives.

The only thing I had to do was run it by the principal and the security office to make sure they knew to let them in the door. I also wanted the principal to stop by and check it out if he had time. I figured he'd love to see his students engaged in a class.

However, his immediate answer was no. He didn't think it was a good idea because he didn't know who these strangers were. I assured him I knew them and that it would be fine. I mean, they are poets after all. Their kind are too busy being magically strange and wonderful to hurt anyone. After hearing me out again, his second and final answer was no. "But sir, they just finished filming *Def Poetry Jam* for HBO!" I said. "Sorry, Reynolds," he responded. "No can do."

I was pissed. I couldn't believe I had to tell the poets they weren't allowed to come into our class. Once again, the kids were heartbroken. However, this time I wasn't going to let it go. This was too important to me, and I refused to let the kids down again. So, I did something that was not in my or their best interest, but it was the only way I could think of for the kids to see the show. At the end of the day, I announced that I would be going to the show: "Tonight

Derrick Brown and his friends will be performing as part of the show Solomon Sparrow's Electric Whale Revival at Circle of Hope on Broad Street. The show starts at seven. I am not allowed to take you. However, I am leaving from the Broadway train stop at five thirty to go to the show. If you can find your way to the show, I will pay for you to get in." These words planted the seed for a series of what I call "super-secret" class trips.

My idea was that if I showed up at the train stop at five thirty and a small handful of my students showed up at the same time and got on the same train and walked to the same place as me, I wasn't actually taking them anywhere. We just happened to go the same way at the same time to the same place. Coincidence, right?

I thought this was brilliant. How could I get in trouble? In my mind, kids would tell their parents they were going to see a poetry performance at a church. It's not like no one would know where they were. Then they would take the train up and hop on the bus to the show, and it would be great.

At the time, the downtown train station in Camden was a hotbed of trouble. Just a block or two away was an open-air drug market, and fights, arrests, and chaos were the norm in the lobby of the station. When my wife and I pulled up to the train stop that night, I could see the crowd of kids from a block and a half away. There had to have been fifty students standing outside with their families. I couldn't believe it. I thought four dudes would show up, and we would have this little experience that everyone else would be sorry they missed. Instead a whole slew of young people crowded the sidewalk outside the train station. As I walked up, kids started introducing me to their parents, and the parents started asking a thousand questions about the time and place and when we would be home. It was madness!

I carefully answered each question and then walked into the station. I saw that none of the kids were moving down toward the train, and when I asked why, the overwhelming answer was that they didn't know how to buy tickets. For the next thirty minutes, I stood in the lobby, taking kids' money and running it through the machine, trying to make sure everyone got the right ticket. As soon as I got a student's ticket, I directed them through the turnstile and down to the train platform. When we finally got everyone downstairs, I had to make sure all of the kids got on the same train at the same time. Entering that train was like being part of a flash mob before flash mobs existed.

Our packed train took us over the Ben Franklin Bridge and into Philly. We got off the train at the Eighth and Market Street exit and climbed the stairs to street level. My original plan had been to take myself and my merry band of explorers on the bus right to the venue, but I was not about to navigate getting fifty students on a public bus. I'd have to help them figure out how to pay, where to sit, and when to get off. Not to mention, it was nearly impossible to get everyone's attention at one time. Most kids looked around wide-eyed at all of the buildings and people, and while they would move wherever the mass would move, they weren't particularly paying attention to me. I was pressed to make a decision, so I decided we would just start walking in the direction of City Hall and I'd think of something on the way. In the few blocks it took to get to City Hall, I didn't come up with an alternative to walking, so like Forrest Gump, we just kept going.

I called the venue to let them know I was coming with a large number of kids, but that we had to walk, so we would be very late. For the better part of the next hour, my fifty or so students and I walked two-and-a-half miles to Circle of Hope in South Philly. We took over the sidewalk, and one of my students, Dykyra, said hello to everyone we passed. They delayed the show over an hour for us, and when we arrived, poetry mastermind Mike McGee walked up to me and gave me a giant hug. Our crew was already a hit. Everyone had heard we were on our way, and folks were outside waiting to see us roll up.

Our mob rolled in thick, and we got everyone seated. As we waited for the show to begin, Derrick Brown asked if I had any students who would be willing to open the show. He thought it might be a fun way to get the kids into what was happening and to give their talent a spotlight. So, to a crowd of about one hundred strangers, Danny Cortez, Caprice Accosta, and Christina Torres stood up and delivered poetry that had never before been heard. They each took turns sharing from notebooks and from memory the verses they had written alone in their rooms with a crowd that was eager to listen. It was a magnificent sight to see these brave and vulnerable kids in the front of the room as they became a part of the show.

The next two hours were just incredible. Derrick Brown, Buddy Wakefield, Anis Mojgani, and Mighty Mike McGee killed it, and even those who would never have otherwise read or listened to poetry became converts to the power of words. After the show, I rounded up the crew and walked the two-and-a-half miles back to the train station, and the train took us back over the bridge to Camden. The night was an incredible success. The next day at school everyone was talking about the train, the walk to the show, the kids performing, and the incredible and moving poems they heard. What I hadn't expected was how different the kids would be in class from then on.

DERRICK BROWN POETRY SHOW

To my knowledge, none of the kids had ever done anything remotely like that. They'd never gone to the city. They'd never been to a poetry show. They'd never been on such a makeshift excursion. The kids knew that this was not how school operated but that their teacher thought it was important enough for them to experience that he was willing to go for it.

After that trip, I never had a problem in class with any of the students who went with me. It was as if I had paid the price of admission into their hearts. Overnight, my room became one of the spots to hang out before and after school. Kids started coming in to eat lunch with me. Best of all, I had more buy-in from the class than I had ever had before. The Harlem Renaissance project was next-level that year, and this was also the class that transformed our classroom into the Globe Theatre to perform *Romeo and Juliet*. From that time on, we took a number of other class trips—some official but mostly super-secret—going everywhere from Princeton University to Eastern State Penitentiary. More than anything, this experience showed me that my students would go hard in class if I met them halfway. If we want our students to put in hard work and to think outside the box, we need to be willing to do the same. In fact, we need to be willing to go far beyond what we ask our students to do. Teachers need to be the example of what we want to see in our students.

Life-Changing Experiences: VaynerMedia

In the spring of 2017, I was watching the *#AskGaryVee Show* on YouTube as I was editing a new video for my channel. Gary Vaynerchuk is the CEO of VaynerMedia, a $150-million-a-year media company in New York City. You can watch the first ten minutes of any speech he does to get his back story, but the SparkNotes version is that Gary is an entrepreneur who, at the age of four, moved to the

United States from the former Soviet Union with his family. After almost failing out of high school, he began working in his father's liquor store in Edison, New Jersey. Over the course of ten years, Gary took his father's liquor store from $2 million a year in sales to over $60 million a year. At 35, he handed his father's business back to him and started a digital marketing firm, even though he knew nothing about digital marketing. That company also exploded. Besides just running the day-to-day operations of VaynerMedia, Gary also began creating YouTube content to document his daily life as well as to help other would-be entrepreneurs grow their businesses.

I'd been watching Gary for about a year when I began to occasionally show his videos to my classes as well. They were always a hit. Something about the way Gary speaks lets you know he's not trying to swindle you or deceive you in any way. He is simply trying to share very simple and practical advice. I think that was one reason I was drawn to him, too. Similar to my hero Rafe Esquith, Gary thinks that working hard and being nice will get you further than being a jerk and cheating people.

For the previous few months, I had been sending in questions whenever Gary did his live show. Regardless of what I was doing when I got a notification that the show was on—doing the dishes, editing YouTube content, or even driving down the highway—I would stop, tune in, and ask my question. My question was always the same: "What advice would you give high school seniors who don't know what's going to happen after senior year?"

Every year my fellow teachers and I are concerned about some of the seniors. Kids who don't know what's next. Graduation? Military service? The working world? The streets? Many of the guys I teach come from single-parent homes where mom and grandma are holding down two jobs each just to keep things going. Many of my students do not have fathers who are around, and most of them will be the first in their families to graduate high school. Their families are thrilled to watch these young men work their way through high school and go onto college, experience things they never did, and build lives that get them away from the streets. The streets are a tricky place though. They are like the Sirens from *The Odyssey*. You can try to leave, but they are always calling you back. In Philly, you are expected to rep your block. For better or for worse, you are expected to be there when someone on your block needs you. Young people feel they have little choice in the matter. If someone from another street disses a guy you barely know on your block, you are expected to stand by him when he retaliates. The biggest problem with this, of course, is that you get called into dangerous situations, and our school and community have seen too many of these situations turn deadly.

Sam was all about that life. Sam was late to school every day. By his own admission, he couldn't focus or function without getting high in the morning. He repeated the ninth grade twice, barely squeaking by. I had talked to Sam more times than I can count. My colleagues and I were always trying to help him see what was next in life. Where would he go? What would he do? How could we help Sam to keep moving the needle in the right direction so he could, in fact, graduate from high school and live a life he chose instead of just accepting the hand he had been dealt?

I wasn't the only one having these conversations with Sam. A lot of love was being directed at the kid, but all of it just seemed to fall by the wayside. Sam definitely heard what we were saying, but some students just don't want to believe you. They can't let those words permeate their front because to let in that encouragement would be to let down their guard. Vulnerability lets love in, and love puts you on the hook. Vulnerability forces you to admit that sometimes other people know us better than we know ourselves. Worst of all, letting that encouragement and love in might make you start to believe in yourself, and that's a slippery slope. When a student has confidence in themselves, when they have faith in what they are capable of, their only option is to do the work—the hard work of becoming who you are meant to be. This isn't just a student thing either. Teachers don't want to let this stuff in either. Instead we'd rather blame the school, the students, the administration, the class sizes, the lack of supplies, or whatever else we're allowing to hinder us instead of just looking at ourselves. We are all capable of making something from nothing, but more on that later.

One day I was editing a video, and a notification popped up that Gary was going live on YouTube. I stopped what I was doing and swiped the notification. As we watched the live feed, my wife and I simultaneously typed in the same question. As luck would have it, Gary's guest that day was Adam Braun, the founder of the nonprofit Pencils of Promise. I found out later that one of Gary's team saw my question and thought it was a good fit because Adam was there to talk about his education initiative. While watching the live feed, my phone started ringing. It was a New York phone number. I didn't put two and two together at first. I'd been sending this question in for ages with no results, so when the number popped up, I just assumed it was someone else. When I answered the phone, I heard, "Yo! It's Gary Vee, and you're on the *#AskGaryVee Show* with Adam Braun. What's your name?!"

"What?! I can't believe this!"

"I'm not joking!"

What happened next was so surreal that it still boggles my mind. As educators we often get used to handling things on our own or with the small communities of educators we have become a part of. Asking for help from the district or the outside world often leads to nothing. So, when I asked my question, and Gary said, "Hey Reynolds, can I ask you a question? If I paid for the bus, like I know schools are fucked up [but] could you bring like eight or nine of them up here to hang with me for an hour?," I didn't know what to say. Like many of you, I teach at a school that is underfunded. One hundred percent of my students get free or reduced-priced lunch. Walking to and from school is a dangerous business for students. In

West Philly, we dream on a budget and are in the business of making something from nothing. So, when the CEO of a multimillion-dollar business asks if you and your students can come and visit his offices in New York City for the day, it stops you in your tracks. I told Gary we would love to come to New York City for the day. Gary's assistant Tyler called me and we picked a date and time, and then all that was left for me to do was pick which students would go with me.

The students I picked to go on the trip were a real mix. Some guys like Danzler and DJ Dirty Kev come from homes with loving parents but I thought could grow even more from a trip like this. They are the kind of young men who already have a fire lit inside them. I thought an experience like this would help to pour gasoline on their flames. Some of the other students I picked were kids I was deeply concerned about. My colleagues and I were not sure where these young men would go after high school, and this trip was a chance for them to step out of their normal lives and be a part of something that was potentially life changing.

The day of our trip, my wife and I, my friend Younkers, who heads up our Special Education Department, and ten excited dudes got on a bus sent by VaynerMedia to head to New York City for the day. The boys were ecstatic. The bus had two flat-screen TVs and a bathroom with a real wood door. "Reynolds, this bathroom has a real door!"

"What did you expect, bro? A sheet?"

"Nah, man, usually they have those flimsy foldy doors? This motherfucker is real wood!"

Many of my students had never been to New York City before. Many rarely left their own neighborhoods in Philly. Everyone was glued to the bus windows as we rolled through Manhattan. It's always a joy to see the boys be boys, to see them momentarily drop the front and look at the world around them in wonder.

When we exited the bus, we were met by Gary's assistant and right-hand man, Tyler. Tyler took us inside the skyscraper at Hudson

Yards and gave us a rundown of where we were and what we would be doing that day. As we walked into this enormous glass building, we were asked to place our bags on a conveyor belt and walk through a metal detector. Everyone but Sam did so. Sam did not want his bag searched. He instead walked over to Ms. Younkers.

"Yo, Yonk. I can't have them search my bag."

"It's mandatory. They do it to everyone. What's wrong?"

"I have weed on me."

Every time I tell this story, I feel that I'm being judged. However, it was one of those moments where, as a teacher, I was faced with a decision. Do I take Sam back to the bus? Do I call the principal? What would you do? I brought this kid on purpose to give him an experience that might hopefully change his life. It was already a Hail Mary situation, and, in fact, I was asked by more than one teacher why I would bring a guy like Sam. Many thought it was a waste to take a kid with no direction who might not even take the situation seriously.

Younkers then came to me and told me what was going on. My reaction was the same as hers.

"Bro! Why did you bring weed with you? Did you think we were going to party on the bus? I can't do that, my kid's gotta eat! Put it in your pocket."

"I can't. I have *a lot* of weed."

Sam held out his hands to show us that he had about a small lettuce-sized bag of drugs with him.

"Dude! What in the world were you thinking?!"

"Ren, I couldn't just leave it anywhere. I was afraid it would get stolen, and I'm responsible for it."

In the moment, I wasn't sure what the right move was. This had definitely not been covered in any professional development or college class. In the end, we shoved the bag into my wife's purse, which was not searched, got on an elevator, and headed up to the twenty-eighth floor. My plan was to proceed with the day and then handle the weed issue when we got back to school. I felt like Charlie walking into Willy Wonka's chocolate factory. We had this golden opportunity, and I didn't want my boys to miss out on what could possibly be because of Sam's decision.

As we stepped off the elevator, we were met by one of Gary's team. He walked us all around the floor of VaynerMedia. My students looked around and were amazed by what they saw. You wouldn't know this to look at them, however, because the front was up. You see, our guys don't show their cards until you have established trust. They can't let you know what they're thinking. One homie on the trip, Frozone, nicknamed that because of striking resemblance to the character from the movie *The Incredibles*, is one of the nicest kids you could imagine. He's the kind of kid who hugs me every day, who is always asking if he can help with anything, or who will just stop in my classroom to see how I'm doing. Frozone walked through that office with a face so hard you would have never known what was in his heart at the moment, but about halfway through the tour, he cracked. As we were walking through one of the creative departments, Frozone walked up to one of the employees and politely asked her what she was working on. The young woman's face lit up like she was so excited about what she was doing that she couldn't wait to explain it. She was working on an ad for Pinterest and took the time to explain to Frozone what program she was using and how they came up with the design. Shortly after, we were called over by another group of women working together.

"Come here, y'all!"

My boys skeptically went over.

"Where are you all from?"

"Philadelphia."

"Do you all want some free samples?"

"What?! Sure!"

The boys were all then given samples of high-end lotions and shampoos. They graciously took them and said thank you. This was our experience for the duration of our time at VaynerMedia. I've taken my students on a lot of trips over the years. We have traveled domestically and abroad, and when traveling with a group of young black and brown men, the looks we get in most places are pretty consistent. We are typically met with more skepticism and anxiety than excitement and courtesy. The people who work at VaynerMedia could not have been kinder and more welcoming. It felt very strange, while also being a huge relief. Everyone we met in the office that day took the time to stop what they were doing and talk to our students about what they did and how they did it. It was clear that VaynerMedia's culture of kindness was not some ruse on YouTube. It was an authentic expression that made me and my boys feel a bit more at home.

Despite all of this, my boys were still on full fronting mode. In a conference room right next to Gary's office, we were shown a large buffet of food and told that it would be a few minutes before Gary would meet with us. In those minutes, with no cameras on us, the boys opened up. They filled their plates and took a hundred selfies against the backdrop of New York City. The conference room was on the corner of the building, so two of the four walls were giant windows looking out on Manhattan. Out one window you could see the Statue of Liberty, and the other provided a glimpse of One World Trade Center.

I had no idea what to expect when Gary came in. To my knowledge, my students didn't know much about him aside from what I'd shown some of them in class. He walked in the room and greeted everyone and was right into the conversation without so much as a moment of social pleasantries.

"Do you guys know who I am?"

Everyone sat silently, waiting. You can watch this whole video on Gary's YouTube channel, but to give you a glimpse, Gary shared his thesis that the chip on your shoulder is actually a superpower. That where you grew up and the hits you've taken can actually empower you instead of crush you. That the same mindset that it takes to be a good drug dealer is what it takes to be a great entrepreneur. This got a huge laugh from my boys.

Gary's response was: "Look at my man Moose (Gary's friend in college). He's breaking down these bags into nickels because he's making more money that way. . . . He's actually making three dollar bags because he realizes everyone at the school doesn't notice the difference and doesn't care. He's smart. And then I'd see other people that would buy like an ounce and smoke fucking three-fourths of it in four minutes and be bad at flipping it, and I'd think, 'He's a fucking loser.' So, if you're good at it, if somebody's good at it, they'd be even better at flipping sneakers or gear or going to the thrift store and flipping because it's the same fucking move. And then, when you have the freedom of being not scared to get caught, now you're fucking moving fast, because when you're selling drugs you got to think about that extra dimension of getting caught. But when you're selling fucking T-shirts, now you're an entrepreneur, and people are putting you on a pedestal."

As soon as Gary said this, my man DJ Dirty Kev opened his arms and hugged Gary and told him he loved him. That was it. Almost an hour into our meeting, some of the wall came down.

We ended the meeting, and Gary took the time to take selfies with everyone and to sign copies of his newest book for each kid. He even went so far as to push his next meeting back to be able to do one-on-one discussions with my guys. It was quite a moment. If you've ever watched Gary's YouTube vlogs, you know that dude works every minute of every day and doesn't stop for so much as a drink of water or to pee. He did, however, stop to make each kid feel seen and heard. I don't know that he'll ever know what that meant to me.

When Gary finally had to leave for his next meeting, we were taken into another room where it was just us. The cameras left, and we were alone to digest and discuss what had just happened. In that

room, the boys sat around the long conference table, again surrounded by glass walls and skyscrapers, and I asked, "What did you
think? What was your takeaway from all of this?" Before anyone
could speak up, Sam said, "I got something." What Sam said next was
the stuff that teachers dream about hearing their students say.

TRIP TO VAYNERMEDIA
TO MEET GARY VEE

"Like I don't even think I could leave here and go back outside
and do the same dumb stuff . . . On a serious note, like I don't think
I could literally go home today and go back outside and do dumb
stuff. Like all I'm thinking about right now is how am I gonna better
myself. Like real rap. I didn't know that would happen to me, bro. I'm
hardheaded, bro. I don't listen to nobody."

I asked Sam, "So what was it then?"

He looked all around the room and pointed his finger and said:
"I never seen this before. You feel what I'm sayin'? I got the talk, I
mean Ms. Younkers talk to me every day, you talk to me every day,
but it's like I see y'all every day. I still connect with y'all but seeing

what I can accomplish if like I just stay in my lane. Like I don't need *this*, but I can definitely better myself, like be a better Sam. I wasn't trying to be a better Sam before. I just didn't care. But now I care. I care what I do. You know what I'm sayin'?"

When you're a teacher, you spend your days doing whatever you can to help students realize and meet their potential. You spend countless hours talking and motivating. You come into school early and stay long after the last bell. You plan special projects to help create student engagement and real-world learning. You make sure your classroom is a place where magic can happen and relationships can be forged. When you and your community literally give all of yourselves so that someone else can grow and have a shot only to realize that your collective efforts are far less than what's needed, it is a crushing blow. We as educators must realize, however, that we are not the be all and end all when it comes to our students succeeding. We are not always what is needed. This doesn't mean some kids are without hope! On the contrary, I believe every child will respond to the right message from the right messenger. We, as teachers, just need to be humble enough to step aside and let someone step in who can get the job done. I believe with all my heart that if the kids *see* it, they can *be* it, and that often it's not the message but the messenger that is most important. That afternoon Sam saw what was possible. He saw a successful man take time out of his day to be hospitable to him and to share his story, a man who had no ulterior motives. Sam left that meeting changed. He went back to Philly and graduated from high school. Just before graduation, he applied for college and, to his great surprise, was accepted. He currently attends college in Ohio. He wanted to be as far away from the call of the street as he could. Sam spends all of his time either in the library or in his dorm room.

When I talk to him now, he always tells me how dark it is on campus at night. "Yo, Ren, it's kind of scary up here. It's so dark."

"Bro, are you kidding me? You used to spend nights working the streets of West Philly. What could possibly happen up there? Is a moose gonna jump out and get you?!"

To me, Sam is a reminder of what is possible when we don't give up. For five years, I knew this dude. I watched him get in trouble again and again. I watched a faculty of committed, caring people rally around him and try to give him their all. And then in one quick swoop, the right messenger at the right moment stepped in and unknowingly did the trick. He cracked the front, which allowed the seed of hope and confidence to take root.

Life-Changing Experiences: Mac Premo and the Brooklyn Circus

'Bril slept every day in my class during his freshman year. I'm not certain I could have identified him in the hallway without looking at the back of his head. He never did work, spoke to no one, and never got excited about anything. To be fair, it had been a tumultuous year in our class. We had a number of kids who had a hard time keeping it together in school. Until that year, I had never had a full-fledged fight in my classroom, but I had several that year. By January, I was on my third co-teacher. The first one went to lunch on the first day of school and never returned. The next hire lasted until winter break. The third hire was a returning faculty member, my friend Ms. Younkers. She and I were determined to make the best out of what looked like a failing year.

Our most difficult class of the day was 'Bril's napping class. On her first day back at our school, I gave Younkers the lowdown on each kid. 'Bril was a hard dude to admit to because I had tried everything I could think of, but he just slept. It's hard to concede that you're not sure what to do with a child when they don't respond. I had called home. I had spoken with administration. I had tried to get the scoop from his friends. Nothing worked. We were at a standstill.

Younkers had been on the trip to meet Gary Vee with me. She had seen firsthand what can happen to a student who has the right messenger, with the right message, at the right time. She and I decided to try to create more opportunities for the students in our classes to hear from influential professionals who were passionate about the work they did.

One of my greatest takeaways from meeting with Gary Vaynerchuk and his team was the way we got there in the first place. No other school has had the opportunity to walk into a boardroom with Gary and his staff and have unlimited free access to them. How did our small school from West Philly end up among the clouds in Manhattan? Simple: we asked. My wife and I probably made hundreds of phone calls over a series of months. We called from the kitchen, from the side of the highway, and while food shopping. I didn't ask for money or time or a handout. I simply asked for advice, and that was the knock that got us in the door.

After our New York trip, Younkers and I began DMing everyone we could think of to see who we could meet up with or get to come and visit our classroom. A DM, or direct message, is a way to send a private message to anyone you are following on Instagram. The beauty of the DM is that it's a white space. It's a way of connecting with people you would never otherwise have the opportunity to talk to. If I had called or emailed any of the people who have visited our classroom over the last few years, I might have never gotten a response because they're overwhelmed with people trying to hit them up by phone or email. The DM is a new way for me to level the playing field for my students in terms of learning opportunities.

One of the people I was lucky enough to connect with was Mac Premo, an American artist and "stuff maker." He is a hero to me and is often the focus of our Weird Friday segments in our classroom. Mac has an incredible workshop at the Invisible Dog Art Center in New

York City. From there, he has created skateboards out of discarded spackle buckets, an art installation from a dumpster, commercials, photography, and set designs that have won him seven New York Emmy Awards. He also collaborated with picture book artist Oliver Jeffers to create a music video for U2's "Ordinary Love." One night, as I was dreaming about who would make a great guest for our class, I decided to take a shot and DM Mac Premo.

"Hi, Mac. My name is CJ Reynolds. I'm a high school teacher in West Philadelphia. I've been following your work and showing your videos in my ninth-grade classes for the last few years. My students and I make videos for my YouTube channel, and we were wondering if you were available to meet up. If that sounds like too much, I'd love the chance to sit down with you for ten minutes and ask you some questions and film it so I could show my students. Thanks for all the great work that you do."

There it is, short and sweet. A few days later I got a message back saying, "Hi, CJ. Thanks for the message, and I'm flattered that you're sharing my work with your students. What are you thinking in terms of a meetup?" Mac then invited us up to Brooklyn to hang out and create something together in his studio. That fall, I picked a handful of kids, loaded up the school van, and headed back to New York City for another meetup.

The students I chose this time were what I refer to as "special flowers." Special flowers are students who don't quite fit into the mold of the average high school kid. The kids who choose puppet making, skateboarding, or anime over football. The kids who listen to hardcore or '80s metal music rather than hip-hop. These kids always have my heart because I feel like that was me back in high school. I looked like everyone else, but my interests were not always the same as my peers. I eventually found my crew in high school, and as a teacher I try to make connections between kids who I can see are special flowers like I was.

Every trip has a number of kids who I know will be able to walk away with a positive experience. Again, these are the students whose preexisting fires I'm trying to fuel up. All of my trips also involve kids who are wild cards. Wild cards are students who I'm not sure will take anything away from the trip, but, as with Sam, I'm willing to do anything to help them realize their potential. The wild card of the kids on this trip was 'Bril. I wasn't even sure if he would want to go, but I knew I wanted him to. I'm not sure what got him to say yes—it could have been that his friends were all going or the mere fact that he was invited somewhere—but 'Bril ended up taking the ride with us to New York City and having his life changed in ways Younkers and I couldn't have seen coming. When we arrived at the Invisible Dog Studio, we called Mac and told him we had made it. As we waited for him to come downstairs, a well-dressed African American man came up to me on the sidewalk and asked if my name was CJ. I said it was, and he told me his name was Ouigi Theodore and he was the owner of a menswear boutique called The Brooklyn Circus. He said Mac had invited him to come and hang with us for the day. Ouigi then invited us to visit his store later that afternoon to give the boys a view of what it was like to run a business.

Mac took us into the Invisible Dog, which got its name because it was formerly the factory where they made those dog leashes that made it look like you were walking an invisible dog. We were introduced to the founder and director, Lucien Zayan. To get to Mac's shop, we rode up on an old freight elevator that still had images painted on it from when U2 had filmed their "Ordinary Love" video there. Walking into Mac's space set off an endless stream of questions. His creator space looks like Thomas Edison and Pee-wee Herman shared an office. Mac showed the boys a machine he was creating. He called it the 6-4-3 machine, named for the scorebook numbering system for a double play from shortstop to second base to first base. "Did you get hired to make this thing?" one of the students asked.

"Nope. I just built it because I wanted to."

"Sir, why would you build this giant complicated machine without doing it for money?"

"Well, I love baseball and just wanted to create a double-play machine and put it in a room."

This idea of making something simply because it is in you and you need to get it out was a theme for the rest of the day, and it has been a motivator ever since for the students who heard it. To meet a man who has found great success in creating art and who spends the balance of his time creating plays, art, and video content just for the joy of doing it shifted the needle for many of our students, especially 'Bril.

"What's that?" someone asked Mac.

"Those are silk-screen frames that I used to create T-shirts and pennants."

"You made your own T-shirts?"

"Yeah, man. I just design what I want it to say or be and then I make these silk-screen frames and print them."

"Can we make a shirt?"

"Yeah, let's do it. What one do you want to make?"

For the next hour, my students made shirts by squeezing paint onto silk-screen frames and then pressing it onto shirts. Mac also took the time to walk them through how he came up with the idea for his bucket boards.

"On every job site in the world, you find hundreds of these buckets that get used one time and then are just thrown in the garbage. I thought, why couldn't we make something cool out of them? I called a friend of mine who makes custom skateboards and asked him if we could incorporate the buckets into a skateboard design and we did it."

Mac patiently answered every question the students had. He let them get their hands dirty and make something and allowed them to roam free and look at everything with their hands. Everyone left the shop that day with a shirt or two they had made themselves and a skateboard deck, but beyond that, they left with the sense that if they wanted something—a shirt, a skateboard, an idea to come to life—they might just be able to make it themselves. I've said it before, but our school dreams on a budget. We don't have a lot of money, but necessity is the mother of invention, and showing kids that they have power can ignite in them a flame that is nearly impossible to extinguish. Look, I'm aware that on the surface my boys made a few projects that many had made before them. It wasn't rocket science. But I also know that momentum is an amazing thing. If you point a student in a direction that fascinates them and give them a little push, you just might set off a chain reaction of events that changes that child's life forever.

Later that afternoon, we walked a few blocks away and visited The Brooklyn Circus. Ouigi welcomed my boys into his design space and showed them how he designed and made all of his clothes. He walked them through how he picked fabrics and where he got his inspiration. He showed them the difference between well-made buttons and the buttons most of us have on our clothes. He explained,

MEETING UP WITH MAC PREMO IN BROOKLYN

"The references are *Cooley High*, sports, Jay-Z Brooklyn, Spike Lee Brooklyn."

When we walked into the store itself, we were greeted by Ouigi's team. All of the young men who were working that afternoon showed us around the boutique and let the boys touch and look at anything they liked.

"Bro! This T-shirt is eighty dollars!"

"Ouigi, why is this jacket five hundred and fifty dollars?!"

Ouigi explained that he ran his business by what he called the hundred-year plan. "We create clothes, culture, and lifestyle that will ultimately last. I feel like in one hundred, two hundred, five hundred years of African American history, we've preserved our pain and other things that affect us up to this day, but I don't think we put enough value on the things that we've made and created. I want The Brooklyn Circus to become the vintage of the community."

Just like in Mac's studio, we were never rushed. We were welcomed in and treated as guests. The boys tried on gear and sat in the back of the store taking turns trying on Ouigi's PRICE headphones. It made me nervous just looking at those headphones. These boys are so rough with everything that they've broken every pencil sharpener I've ever had in my room. The employees walked the boys through why the store was set up the way it was and how important details were in everything they did from folding shirts to knowing your customers. All of the students left that day with an official Brooklyn Circus T-shirt and a spirit that was soaring.

Unfortunately, we're limited in who we can be for our students. I can give them my time, attention, advice, and know-how, but at the end of the day I'm a straight white man from Haddon Heights, New Jersey. I don't know what it's like to grow up as a young black man. I can read every book by Ta-Nehisi Coates, listen to every Kendrick Lamar album, and surround myself with urban African American culture, but at the end of the day I am still who I am. I find power in knowing my own limitations. It forces me to reach beyond myself, and it reminds me that I am not the end all and be all in the lives of my students. When I look at teaching from that angle, I am free to reach out to my community and ask for help. At The Brooklyn Circus, that help came in the form of my students seeing someone who looked like them, talked like them, and came from a similar starting point transcend his limitations and create a business, community, and lifestyle that most folks only dream about. It was a reminder that if you see it, you can be it. Ouigi had grown up in Port-au-Prince, Haiti. He

BROOKLYN CIRCUS TRIP

now owned and operated a designer menswear boutique that was world renowned and visited by every imaginable hip-hop mogul. He is a contributing member of his community. He employs young people and shows them the ropes of running a business that focuses on legacy. Ouigi Theodore is the kind of man who happily puts his business on hold to spend the day with kids he has never met before just to be an example for them. I can't be that example for my boys, but I can make the connection and drive the van to get them there.

Schools are built for vanilla children. Teachers need to create learning and growing situations for kids that are rocky road and mint chocolate chip as well. It is of crucial importance that we provide all students examples of someone who looks like them, feels like them, thinks like them, or has come from the same starting point as them. Gay, straight, Hispanic, artsy, autistic, nerdy, Black, transgender, poor, athletic, introverted, dyslexic, gifted, physically or mentally disabled . . . Seeing someone who is the same flavor as you do things that seem impossible for your flavor suffocates excuses and helps students see what is possible.

I understand that it seems implausible to finish this story by saying that since that day 'Bril has been a different kid. But the fact of the matter is that, after almost a year of sitting with his head down, a day in Brooklyn with the right people made the difference. He has come alive in school and begun living out loud. Every morning, 'Bril and his crew pile into my classroom and store their skateboards and jackets in the corner. They started recording music together in my classroom after school and made plans to create a clothing company. So much happens in my classroom on any given day that it's hard to sometimes keep track of what everyone is up to, but a year and a half after meeting with Mac and Ouigi, 'Bril came to me at the end of the day and asked if he could use my room to run interviews after school.

"Of course, bro. What are you interviewing for?"

"I'm interviewing students who want to be a part of my company."

I then watched as students came into my room and 'Bril carefully asked them what they thought they could bring to his empire. It was inspiring and heartwarming.

We all have students who walk reluctantly into our classrooms and schools every year. Students who want nothing to do with what we are doing in the classroom. Kids who have lost hope in the education system and in themselves. These are the students for whom we must think outside the box. Mac and Ouigi had nothing to gain by having us visit them. They were also two perfect examples of what could be done with a life when you are not afraid to follow your dreams and to work hard. Neither of those gentlemen said anything very different to 'Bril and the boys than my fellow teachers and I had been saying for years. What they did offer was an opportunity for my students to leave their everyday lives and step into a world that allowed them to see what their own lives could be. Our meeting with Mac and Ouigi allowed my boys to ask, "What if?" What if I started a podcast? What if I designed my own T-shirts to sell? What if I made my own music or artwork? When we find experiences to disrupt the norm and help our students see and experience what is possible, we give our students the greatest of gifts—the ability to dream wildly big, audacious dreams and the courage to see them come alive.

 ## REAL RAP:

HELP STUDENTS WIDEN THEIR CIRCLE OF INFLUENCE

Bringing guests into your classroom and taking trips to visit new locations can empower, uplift, and motivate your students, and it is one of the best ways to create a classroom culture that goes beyond test scores and participation points. It builds the intrinsic motivation we all long for our students to have.

It's also important to note that not every guest who visits your classroom needs to look like your kids. They just need to be able to be real and relatable. We've had men, women, entrepreneurs, comic book creators, hip-hop artists, graffiti artists, and CEOs enter our classroom, and it has made all the difference. It is real-world learning in a way that I could never have done on my own. Some of the biggest changes in our students have resulted from the kindness of strangers who have been willing to share their time and knowledge. These experiences have built real connections between my students and professionals who are the best at what they do. It has widened the circle of influence for my students and shown them an alternative to what they see on the streets every day. If we are indeed the average of the five people we hang with the most, then what better gift can we give our students than to help them widen their circle of influence in hopes that the seeds of greatness are planted and watered.

How do you go about picking the people and places you want to share with your students? Like so many other things in education, it requires knowing who your students are, what they're interested in, and what they need to make the correct choices. Once you know what it is that lights your students up, you will have an idea of who you might connect with. When I contacted Mac Premo through Instagram DM, I knew he would be a good fit because he was an artist who had figured out a way to make money while still creating the art he loved. I also knew that skateboarding had changed his life when he was a kid. He said that skateboarding made him see things differently. Every curb became an opportunity. I hoped that Mac would be able to inspire some of my students who move on the edges of our school community, the kids who sometimes feel they don't fit in. I wanted them to see someone who made a living on the fringe and wore his differences like a badge of honor.

When I contacted Gary Vaynerchuk through YouTube, I knew he had grown up hating school, was an immigrant with learning disabilities, and had to figure out a way to make his particular skill set work for him. As I said before, Gary seemed to be the perfect messenger for students who had no idea what was next in their lives as well as students who had already at their young age been beaten down by life. My dream was to have Gary light a fire in them and help them see that you really can make something from nothing.

When the Philly street artist Amberella came into my classroom, I knew she'd be able to speak to my students about mental health and entrepreneurship. Amberella has made a living creating a particular type of street art by a practice called wheatpasting. She hangs her signature black-and-white hearts all over the city. Each heart has a message for those who pass by: "Can't stop. Won't stop"; "Ur all you need"; "You got this. Keep going." When she visited our classroom, she spoke to my boys about how she created these mantras as a reminder to herself that she was powerful and loved. Amberella was able to speak right to the heart of my students, who themselves need a daily reminder of how incredible they are, kids who sometimes feel invisible and aren't sure what to do with their pain.

The next step is to look at what you are trying to teach in class and how you might connect it to another place or person. When my students and I were reading *Night* by Elie Wiesel, I knew we didn't have the money to go to Washington, DC, to visit the US Holocaust

STREET ARTIST AMBERELLA POSTING HER ART IN OUR CLASSROOM

Memorial Museum or have a speaker come and meet with us. Instead we planned a visit to Eastern State Penitentiary, a former prison a few miles from our school. The prison is a haunting and decrepit building. If I wanted my students to get a sense of how it feels to have your life and your dignity stripped from you, we would take a trip to one place near us that was known for doing just that. I reached out to the prison through email and asked if they could provide us with a free tour. They agreed, and the students had a memorable and surreal experience walking the halls and stepping into the cells of former prisoners. When we were back in the classroom reading *Night*, we were able to draw comparisons with the cold, hard conditions of the prison cells we visited.

When our hip-hop class was studying symbolism and the power of word choice, I connected with a local graffiti artist through Instagram. He met me and my boys in Center City in Philadelphia and gave us a tour of the alleyways and backstreets that had some of his favorite graffiti tags. My boys were given an opportunity to think about what words and images they would want to represent them. Then they were given T-shirts, and we used different spray paint cans and nozzles to craft art they could wear.

Another year, our students were studying children's books as a way of understanding how short stories and pictures can work together to tell a story. To help build excitement around the activity, my co-teacher Ms. Younkers reached out to her friend, Reggie Byers, who is the creative mind behind the *Afroboy* comic. He came into our classroom and spoke to the students about growing up in a tough neighborhood and how he was bullied as a child. As he drew our students in with his stories, he also began drawing the images that accompanied his tale on the white board in the front of the room. Every student was 100 percent engaged and couldn't believe their eyes as Reggie charismatically spoke and drew at the same time, weaving together storytelling and art in a way that made the idea of creating children's books exciting for my teenage students.

All of these experiences and many more were made possible by finding people on social media who I thought were a great fit, asking friends and family if they knew anyone who would be an engaging guest for the class, or posting on social media to see if any of my online friends had a connection. When you send the email, DM, or Twitter message to a potential visitor, I suggest being simple and direct and making it about the students. My typical message is usually along the lines of the following: "Hello, (name of awesome visitor). My name is CJ Reynolds. I teach ninth-grade literature and the History of Hip-Hop in West Philadelphia. My students and I love the work you're doing, and we were wondering if you'd be willing to come and visit us in our classroom one day. If that sounds like too big of an ask, we'd also be happy to meet you through Google Hangouts or Skype. Thanks for all the great work you do. We appreciate you. Peace. CJ Reynolds."

STUDYING GRAFFITI IN PHILLY'S BACK ALLEYS

Teachers, remember that most people don't have the honor of being able to work daily with young people. However, they do know how important the work that you do is. They want to help, to give back, to make the world a better place. When you reach out, remember that you are not just asking for a favor; you are providing folks with the opportunity to plant a seed in your students—a seed that might just change their lives. Dream big! If you could have anyone in the world visit your classroom, who would it be? Message that person and at least ask. As my hero Pat Croce says, "If you don't ask, the answer is always no."

6

CLASSROOM MANAGEMENT

The Reality of Classroom Management

The most frequent questions I get from education students and other teachers are about classroom management. This makes sense, given that when your classroom management is tight, your day goes much better and your lessons much more smoothly. If your management is off, your hair starts turning from brown to white and you start drinking on your lunch break. In this section, I want to give you a clear sense of how I get my students to work efficiently and what I do when they are not. I also want to explain where I have failed in the past, so you can learn from some of my mistakes.

Effective classroom management can't just be planned; it needs to be practiced. When you find the practices that work for you, it will indeed make everything about your classes better—infinitely better. When you don't have it on lock, you'll start thinking things like, "Why does every other teacher have it together and I don't?" "Am

I a failure?" "Was becoming a teacher a mistake?" You have dreams about it. You can't pay attention to dinner conversations because you can't stop thinking about what happened at school—how that kid spoke to you; how that teacher looked at you when she saw your class walking to lunch; how the students just won't listen, stay seated, stop touching each other, take out what is needed, participate, or stop cursing, throwing stuff, and biting each other.

It's easy to beat yourself up about your classroom management, but before you do, let me reassure you of two important ideas. The first is that no one can train you on how to best manage your classroom. Learning classroom management in a college classroom is like learning how to swim in a classroom. You can read about swimming. You can learn the molecular properties and physics of water. You can watch videos to learn the best form while in the pool. You can check out the newest technology and how it can help you be more buoyant and effective in the water. You could even have a professional swimmer come into your class and speak to you about their own best practices. But on that first day of school when you climb the steps of the high dive and jump into the deep end, all of that theory goes right out the window. Now it's time for action.

The second is that how you manage your classroom is based more on who you are as a person than it is on any set of rules or guidelines. For example, in college we were told not to smile until December. Doing so would lead to the kids mistaking your kindness for weakness. So, when I entered my first classroom, I tried that. It lasted two days. I couldn't do it. It's in my DNA to smile and to make others smile. After jumping off the high dive, I learned quickly that being my authentic self in the classroom would serve me better than trying to be something I'm not. Whether you're funny, strict, quiet, disciplined, quirky, silly, or just plain weird, you need to lean into that in the classroom. No single personality type wins more than another. It's about being brave and sharing your true self with your students so they will be brave enough to do the same. How do I show my wacky, weird, authentic personality in the classroom to build engagement and minimize behavior issues? I'm glad you asked.

My Classroom Management Methods

The following are some of the ideas I use in my classroom to get the most out of my time with my students. It's important to remember that what works for me might not work for you. You might not feel comfortable doing these things or your school might not even allow it. In fact, some of the stuff I do should not be replicated by anyone else. Teaching is a lot like cooking. I can share my recipe, but that doesn't mean it needs to be followed to a T. Don't like grilled peaches in your salad? Take them off. Not a fan of Swiss cheese? Switch it up for some cheddar. Want to put grape jelly on your scrambled eggs? Go for it. Having said that, here is a master list of classroom management strategies I use on a daily basis. Hopefully you'll find some easily applicable tips and tricks and some inspiration for what you could do in your classroom.

My room is a safe space. I get to school around 7:20 every morning, even though class doesn't start until 8:05 a.m. Every morning when I get to my door, students are already there, waiting for me. They come to my classroom and eat breakfast, talk about sports, and help me get my room ready for the day. Although I primarily teach ninth grade, the kids who come to hang out are a mix of all grades. Everyone is welcome. My expectation is that you keep my room clean and, like Fonzie said, "be cool." The thing about a safe space is that it is no longer safe if kids are using language that's offensive to one another, teasing each other in a hurtful way, or being too loud and distracting. I'm all for weird, silly, and playful. What I can't get down with is mean, rude, and unhinged. A few years ago, I had a group of LGBTQ students who would hang in my classroom every day. They were a funny crew. They would critique the teachers' outfits and have dance parties in my classroom after school. One morning, one of the crew came in and told me he had a new wig he wanted to show me. He then proceeded to pull a three-foot-long salt-and-pepper-colored wig out of his backpack. He put it on his head and immediately looked like the mom from *The Addams Family*. Someone quickly played music on their phone, and all of a sudden, our room became a cat walk with my man strutting around like it was fashion week. In the midst of this, another group of students walked into my room and were clearly thrown off by what was going on: "Reynolds, what is happening? You get down with this?" I replied that it didn't matter what I "got down with." What mattered was that my students had a safe space to express themselves. "All are welcome here, my man." "Word. I got you, Ren." With that, the new crew came in and sat down for breakfast, and just like that two worlds came together. Remember, it's up to you what happens in this unstructured time. I like to use it as a way to check in with kids, find out the latest news, and allow my students to talk about what's on their minds. I wouldn't start my day any other way.

I shake hands with every kid who enters my classroom. Our school has eight periods a day. During the transition time between each period, you can find me in the hallway talking to kids and shaking the hand of every kid who enters my classroom. I do this for a couple of reasons. One is to show respect. My only classroom rule is "Give respect, get respect." So, before and after each class, I shake hands to show that I respect you. Two, I want every kid to feel seen. No one flies under the radar in my room. If you've met me or even seen me on YouTube, you might find this hard to believe, but I was a pretty quiet and insecure kid in my early high school years. I was the guy the teacher would never remember. My senior year of high school, I was in the library with some friends and someone put a book in my backpack without me knowing about it. When I walked through the exit of the library, the alarm went off, and I got written up for trying to steal a book. My friends thought this was hilarious and howled with laughter as I was sent to the office. When I got there, I was called into the vice principal's office. As she looked over my write-up and began lecturing me on the repercussions of my actions, she said something that has never left me.

"Mr. Reynolds, where did you go to school before transferring to CCVTS?"

"I went to Haddon Heights Middle School."

"No. I mean, where did you go to high school before coming here?"

"Nowhere. I've been here for the last four years."

"That's funny. I don't recognize you. I don't remember seeing you around before."

"And that's exactly why you should let me go. I haven't gotten in trouble since I've been here."

SHAKING EVERY HAND THAT COMES THROUGH MY DOOR

I did get off the hook for my friend's prank, but I remember wondering how in the world she had never noticed me before. I went to a pretty large school, but still. That moment stayed with me, and when I became a teacher, I made sure to let every kid who came into my classroom, whether I taught them or not, know that I saw them. I also made sure they knew they could come to me for anything—help on their homework, lost locker combination, birthday gift ideas for their mom . . . I got them covered.

I tell them what they want to know before they even ask. Every day when my students walk into class, they know exactly what they need to do and what we will be doing before I even tell them. This is because I have the day's agenda neatly written or projected on the whiteboard in the front of the classroom. The agenda lets students know the date, what they need on their desk for the day, each activity we will be doing, approximately how long each activity will take, and what the homework will be that night. Beyond establishing a routine and helping the students know what they should be doing to get ready for class, it also helps to alleviate the stress a lot of my students bring into class. Students who come from very unstable family circumstances, students who are on the autism spectrum, and students dealing with any number of other issues often have anxiety about what is happening that day. This simple act helps to decrease that stress.

I give assigned seats. I know it might sound old school, but I think it helps me manage the classroom and allow students to take ownership over the class. My desks are also in rows. As the year progresses, this changes drastically, but in the beginning of the year when I'm trying to teach kids how and why we are going to be organized as a class, it helps a lot. All of the students are seated alphabetically, and everyone has a number assigned to their desk. The reason for this 1950s-looking situation is simple. One, I share a room with several other teachers. They like the classroom set up like this, so I oblige at the start of each year. Two, students thrive on consistency. Knowing which seat you need to be in at the beginning of class avoids the struggle of trying to find a spot as well as arguments about whose seat is whose. I also let students know that they need to be in their seat by the time the bell rings. Kids who are still walking around lose a point off their grade for the day.

Quick note: I don't like using points as a motivator, to be honest. I'd love it if my students came into my class at the beginning of the year and were intrinsically motivated, so eager to learn that they couldn't wait to get into their seats and get started, but the reality of the matter is that not all students show up that way. As part of my students' classwork grades, they are given four points per day (twenty points per week), and they can lose them for various reasons. I'm a big believer in redemption, though, so students can also have points added on if they do something above and beyond as the day and week progress. It's important to note that just saying the words *points* is often enough to get kids to hustle and get started.

As the students and I get to know one another and our class starts to become more of a community, students are allowed to sit wherever they think is the best fit for them, and daily points go away. This is a level of freedom most of my students have never had before, which isn't a surprise as most classrooms gauge their success on how quiet and still their students are. A loud and moving class is often thought of as an unruly mob that is off task. To help my students make the transition from orderly rows to learners who are free to move about as needed, we have a class discussion. Again, students thrive on consistency, so it's important to make them a part of any changes in the class. In our discussion, we talk about things like autonomy in the classroom, student choice in lessons, learning styles, and the importance of students being proactive in their own learning experience. As we talk, I sit with the students, instead of standing over them or in front of them, and we have a true discussion. I am the facilitator, not the dictator. I usually start the conversation with the question, "What would school look like if it was enjoyable?" The kids share what they wish lessons looked like, how they wish they were treated, and what they would love to learn about. As we conclude the conversation, I tell the students that I will take all of their ideas into account and that they should be ready for some real changes in how our class proceeds. From then on, I do my best to incorporate the changes my students brought up. I announce that they may sit anywhere they'd like in the classroom. Just this simple change makes a drastic positive difference in the behavior of the class. It's a small way to show students that they have been heard and that I care about who they are and how they learn. In my ideal classroom, I would get rid of all of the desks and have a giant *Game of Thrones*–style table in the middle of our classroom where students could have conversations and work on assignments, but our school has limited resources to make such dreams a reality. Instead, we bend our reality to make the best out of it.

I keep class moving. From the time the bell rings to start class to the time it rings to dismiss us, I allow for no downtime. We are like a train that starts moving and doesn't stop for anything until it gets to where it's going—unless someone farts. That always stops everyone. But besides farts or the occasional puking kid, we are full steam ahead. My classes are planned in a way that minimizes or eradicates downtime. Downtime leads to students talking, which leads to distracting others, which leads to more talking or someone shouting "shut up," and before you know it, your class has descended into a scene from *Roadhouse*. I get only forty-two minutes a day with each class, and I want to maximize the learning time that we have. I feel like I owe that to my students and their parents. One of the ways I get kids to keep going is by letting them know on the daily agenda how much time they have for each task. Knowing that they have five minutes to finish the day's journal entry keeps kids moving because they know that, when that five-minute mark hits, I'm moving on to vocabulary, and they'll be behind. If a class is taking longer than normal because they're working hard or putting a lot of thought into what they're doing, I will, of course, push the time back, but if we are particularly rambunctious, I stick right to my schedule, and they get the message quickly.

I manage the most difficult kids in a particular way. Every year we all have at least one—or twenty—kids who are particularly challenging. What do you do with the kids who will not get on board no matter what you've tried? They won't stop talking, touching other people, throwing things, or being generally disrespectful. The thoughts in this section are a combination of ideas I've learned from other teachers over the years. Thanks, Ribay and Major. Your advice changed my life.

The first thing you want to do is stay cool. You can't let kids see that you've lost your cool. Now maybe you've lost your cool on purpose in some sort of calculated explosion, but that's a conversation for later. What I'm talking about is not losing your temper in front of a kid who wants nothing more than for you to start screaming and yelling and spitting and babbling on and on about you calling home or them getting a zero. Instead be cool. Keep it together.

The second thing you do is squat next to—never lean over—the student, then ask them what they are doing or not doing. "Are you refusing to do work? To be clear, are you saying you will not complete the assignment?" By approaching the issue in this way, you are not accusing the student, thereby avoiding a verbal altercation where you say, "Stop talking," to which they reply, "I'm not talking," and you say, "Yes, you were," then they say, "I was asking him a question about the work," and on and on. Instead just ask if you are seeing what you think you are seeing. You're still addressing the situation but in a way that is clarifying and not accusatory. If the behavior persists, I have the following conversation.

"Mr. Walker, when class is over, I'm going to call your home and I want you to know what that call will sound like so you don't get it twisted. 'Good afternoon, Ms. Walker. Today in literature class your son was having a very difficult time staying on task and not touching other students. I asked him three times to stop touching the young man next to him, and each time he refused to stop what he was doing. When I tried to speak with him in the hallway, he refused to talk about it and told me that he didn't do anything wrong and that this was unfair."

I then let the student know that they can prevent that phone call if they will, as my friend Mr. Harrison likes to say, "get [their] mind right." This idea works because it allows the student to see what is coming next if they continue on the course they are currently on. It also gives them the chance to course correct before it's too late.

The final piece of advice in dealing with this kind of student is to always follow up. Never just hand a student over to the dean, the principal, or a security guard without following up. You need to finish what was started in your classroom. It sends the message to the student that you care and that you are not sending them out of class because you can't handle your own business. When I send a student out of my classroom for misbehaving, it is because I can't stop the class to deal with him or her at the moment. It is my last-ditch effort. I send students out because I am trying to maintain a safe, optimal space for the rest of my students to work.

When I do follow up with that student, that conversation sounds something like this: "Hey, man. I'm really sorry things had to go down in class the way they did today. I need you to know that you are important to me and that I want more than anything for you to have the best learning experience you can in my class. I would do anything in my power to help you in any way I can. That being said, I need you to walk away from here knowing that everyone in our classroom is important. Today I think you were mistaking my kindness for weakness, and I can't have that. Tomorrow when you come into class, I need you to be on point. If you need to talk about anything, move your seat, or stand on your head to learn better, we can make it happen, but I will not allow you to sabotage our class. You all are too important to me to let that happen. I want you to know that I think you are perfect. Your behavior sucked today. But you are perfect just the way you are. Are we good?"

Bring in Backup

If you lay it down for a kid with real rap, they will usually respond in a way you won't believe. Sometimes, however, students still don't respond. Maybe a kid thinks you have it out for them. Maybe you are just not the messenger for that child. In these cases, you need to bring in backup. I am blessed to be a part of a community of educators who truly care about one another and our students. When a student's behavior is too much for me to handle in the moment, I usually call on one of two people: the head of our Climate Team, Mr. Meeks, or the ninth-grade dean, Ms. Cho. Mr. Meeks is a six-foot-four African American man who grew up in West Philly and often knows better than most where our students and their behaviors come from. Ms. Cho is a five-foot-four Korean woman from California. The three of us could not come from more diverse backgrounds, but we all deeply care for the kids and are committed to our work. We often work together to help students find their way in difficult times.

Sometimes after having tried everything I can think of to help or communicate with a particular student and nothing seems to be working, I will call on Cho to address that student directly. Cho will make time in her schedule to hear the student out and try to see where they're coming from. It's important to give kids space to speak and to be heard. She will then break down where I was coming from, and they will work to find a solution. After working things through with that student, Cho always follows up with me, and we make a plan to sit down together with the student. This can take as little as five minutes, but again, it sends each child the message that we are working as a team to care for their well-being. Other times, when more is needed than a five-minute meeting, Ms. Cho and I will buy a student lunch after she has met with them, and we talk about what is going on over lunch. On these special occasions, we have the time to get to know the students better and a chance to share a bit of our story as well. In our experience, sharing a meal with a student helps to disarm them, opening up space where we can just talk—not about what they did or how school is going, but about everyday interests. In these moments, we often get a glimpse into who that child really is, where they come from, and what motivates their particular behaviors. It's another reminder that everyone has a story. It helps me to remember that all of my students are fighting a battle I know nothing about.

When working with Meeks, the story is similar. Meeks has a way of communicating with our students that is intuitive and almost poetic. Meeks's magic cannot be learned, and fortunately it doesn't *need* to be learned. We are a team, each of us bringing some gift to the table. If I can't break through to a student, Mr. Meeks will saunter up in the hallway and break down the situation in a way that the students always understand. His presence and the way he respectfully and patiently speaks to children are incredible.

I'd like to note a few ideas here. One, teachers need to be vulnerable enough to reach out to a team member for help. It takes courage to admit that sometimes we are not enough. When you feel the fear of incompetence or weakness, remember that you are choosing to put the student first and not your fears. You are moving from defense to offense to make sure your student has every possible chance of succeeding, even when it might make you feel uncomfortable.

Two, we've all heard the saying, "It takes a village to raise a child." I love this idea. Everyone in my village has different strengths. Some of my team are good at deescalating emotional situations, some are good when a gentle and caring heart is needed, and some can quickly cut through nonsense to deliver the real rap and help a student get back on track. It takes time to figure out who you will want as part of your support group in your school and how you all can help one another be the right team for the kids. It is time well spent, as these individuals will literally bring light to many dark and seemingly hopeless days when you don't have the energy or know-how to deal with a situation. You, in return, will be able to be there for them and help them manage difficult times and celebrate awesome times as well.

Teaching is like being in a band. All of the instruments are lovely in and of themselves. Guitar, bass, drums, piano, and vocals can all be enjoyed solo, but some undeniable magic happens when you mix those sounds together. Mother Teresa said, "None of us, including me, ever do great things. But we can all do small things with great love, and together we can do something wonderful." Take time to find the band that will help you work toward making something wonderful for your school community.

Classrooms Are Based on Relationships, Not Dictatorships

Classrooms should not be run like dictatorships. Teachers are not rulers of their domain. If we want to raise leaders, we need to cultivate leaders. Leave room in your class for asking why, for sharing opinions about ideas, procedures, and concerns. Teach kids that their voice and ideas are important. Help them to understand how important it is to exercise those muscles and to feel confident when doing so. When we can teach our young people to share what is close to their heart respectfully and thoughtfully and then carefully listen to what others say in return, we are raising a community of critical thinkers who will make the world a better place. This can be done in any school at any age. One way I've done this in the past is by having a box in the front of my classroom labeled "Box of Questions." Any student could place an anonymous question in the box during the week and just before the end of class on Friday, I would take a few questions from the box and answer them. In our class, I would answer just about any question. Not much is off the table in our room, but if you don't feel comfortable answering a particular question, just skip it. No one will have any idea. Another way I've made time for questions is by simply asking my classes, "Does anyone have a question about anything? And I mean *anything*." If your students walk in one day and you push your textbook aside and ask this, you will get a response like you wouldn't believe. When kids know they are in a safe space, they feel free to ask even seemingly silly or strange questions. This activity helps students to be curious in a school system that has become so scripted and homogenized that our students can forget what it's like to ask a question about something simply because they're interested in it. Through this simple activity, we show kids that it's fun to ask questions and work through them to find solutions or to further our thinking. The questions that you get will simultaneously crack you up and make you wonder why you didn't think of the same thing before. I've gotten wonderful questions in the past like, "Is water wet?" "Where does cinnamon come from?" "Why is there a little pocket in the top of your jeans pocket?" "Where does the term 'hip-hop' come from?" Sometimes I know the answer, and sometimes we need to look it up together. Either way, we are taking time out just to be curious and to make learning fun.

My final piece of advice about classroom management is that you need to know why you want what you want from your students. Why do you want students to stay in their seats? To work quietly? To be respectful of one another? To put their homework in a particular place? To not sing in the middle of a test? To not throw things across the room into the trash can? The answer cannot be "because I told you so" or "because I'm in charge." A lot of teachers get hung up on the idea that students should speak when spoken to, respect their elders, or do as they are told without question. I do believe that respect is crucial in any relationship, but I also believe students have the right to understand *why* the things we ask of them are important. When a student asks me why we have to study vocabulary words or why we need to spend time reading independently or why they need to be quiet after they finish taking their test, I have an answer.

We study vocabulary to be able to be able to express ourselves at the highest level. Everyone in our classrooms has something important to say and I want them to have every tool possible to be able to construct their story, argument, and opinion. Conversely, I never want words to be the roadblock to you fully understanding someone else's story, argument, or opinion. We read quietly alone to become better readers. Nothing makes you a better reader than reading more. I will buy any book that makes you want to read, and I will let you read it anywhere in our room—on the couch, under your desk, or curled up on the window ledge. I give you time to read your book and space to process what it says. We are quiet after tests because we are learning as part of a community and communities look out for each other. Making noise and fidgeting while someone else is trying to stay focused on their assignment isn't looking out for your community. When you finish your test, help your community do the best they can by being silent.

If I notice a lot of trash on the floor at the end of class, I ask students to help out by picking it up. I simply tell them, "This is our classroom. I know you might not have made the mess, but I'd appreciate it if you helped me get the classroom on point for the next period." A simple ask and explanation works better than a demand. It helps students to feel like they have a say in the matter. This is also a great time to place my trash can in the front of the classroom on a stool or table and see who can make the most "trashketball" shots before the bell rings. Now picking up trash becomes a game and an opportunity to show off a little by making the best shot.

When students know why they are doing any task or being asked to adhere to any rule, they become part of the conversation. Allowing our students to ask why they need to complete the homework or why they need to take algebra helps them to grow up as leaders who question everything and look at the world around them with a curious eye. This practice also helps us as educators think more deeply about why we do some of the things we do. Should we be giving homework? Why are my desks set up in rows? Why is grammar important? Should a student's grade be attached to their behavior?

Our students, just like us, are constantly being barraged with news and information. This simple habit can help us to model what it looks like to hit the pause button on the day to think about why we do what we do.

Teach Like a DJ

Whether it's a block party, house party, birthday party, wedding, roller rink, or club, a great DJ makes all the difference. A great DJ knows how to read the room. They don't trust that the playlist from last night's club gig will work for this afternoon's wedding. They keep their head up to see what moves the crowd. They know that each party is different and no song is a hit with every audience. A DJ with the skills to pay the bills is a conductor, a ringleader, a facilitator. They didn't write the music. They don't own the club. They play the same songs as the next person. But what they do is take the ordinary and make it extraordinary.

Every teacher needs to be the DJ of their classroom because every classroom is like a party. Every kid is someone who wants to be moved and given permission to step on the dance floor. Our lessons need to show that we know our audience and know them well. You can't just look at the school's charter, curriculum, or mission statement; you need to know who your kids are and how they get down.

One of my biggest misconceptions when I started teaching was that I would be able to build my lesson portfolio over my first few years and then take the parts that I felt worked best in the classroom and fine-tune them so that by year four or five I would have created a well-oiled machine that students would be run through—a machine that would help them reach their potential while having fun along the way. I would have done the majority of the planning and work I would ever need to do and could just enjoy the fruits of my labor. This was far from the truth. This was not teaching like a DJ. This was crafting a playlist that I thought would work for every class. I still think teachers should take those first few years to try every crazy magical idea they think of. When you fail, take a closer look at that idea and see what went wrong. If it can't be reworked, then get rid of it. For those that can be reworked, tweak them as needed and try them again. After a few years, you'll have a pile of lessons and activities that worked and a pile of misses.

When you teach like a DJ, you look at your classroom differently. DJs, just like teachers, are masters at the art of making something from nothing. Both of them take limited resources, overcrowded rooms, not enough time, wide differences in style and ability among the people they're serving, strict rules from the authorities, and overly scripted and often boring situations and make something special out of it anyway. But how is it done? How can you help a room full of students with wildly varying learning styles and educational needs find success? The idea of differentiating instruction can be overwhelming for teachers. Here are some strategies I use to create an environment in which all students can find success.

Try flexible seating on a budget. I made a mobile school store for my students a few years back. We were trying to raise money for our first trip out of the United States. I had almost no money to get this idea off the ground, so I built the entire store out of unfinished plywood. It was a simple setup consisting of three plywood boxes that looked like shipping crates. I couldn't find a place in our school to store the crates when they weren't in use, so I put them in the back of my classroom. Without realizing it, I inadvertently built three standing desks. I put simple metal stools behind them, and students who had a difficult time sitting still for an entire class period now had a space to stand and even move around a little bit.

One Wednesday, about ten minutes into an independent reading activity, I looked around the room to see how everyone was doing, and I noticed a student was missing. Muppet is the kind of student you can't help but love. He's kind and wacky in a way that makes him seem like, well, a Muppet. He sings and dances out of nowhere, and he has this unique ability to be his own dude without ever catching flack for it. He loved being at the back of the classroom because he knew the desks were the perfect height for him to stand at. When I walked to the back of the room to see where he might have gone, I realized he was sitting in the box. I was certain he was on his cellphone, but as I sneakily peered around the corner of the crate, I found him engaged in his book. At the end of class, I asked him what he was doing in the box. He told me he liked sitting in there because it helped him to focus. As it turns out, this is a thing. I posted a picture online, and a neurologist messaged me to say that kids often liked small, secluded environments to work in because it made them feel safe and it cut out external stimuli. The simple crates I created became a three-for-one deal—school store/standing desk/secret hideout.

Provide fidgets on a budget. Fidgets can be costly, and I've found that they often lose their luster over time, so I try to provide options that I can change up without breaking the bank. Silly Putty is a great choice. It doesn't stain, it can be used again and again, and when it gets gross, you just throw it away. Pipe cleaners are another easy choice for kids who need something to play with to help them focus. They can twirl them around their fingers or the end of their pencils. If they walk off with them at the end of class, it's never a big deal because I buy over three hundred of them for about seven dollars. Velcro under a child's desk gives kids with sensory issues a place to meet their needs on the low. It's not distracting, and they never have to remember to bring it; it's just waiting for them under their desk every day. A friend of mine uses inexpensive exercise bands to help students in her class expel extra energy while staying seated in

FLEXIBLE SEATING ON A BUDGET

class. She simply ties the exercise band to the bottom of the front two legs of the child's chair. The student can bounce their legs and stretch the band, and it's silent as can be. While a lot of teachers will hand out rubber bands, I have found that giving teenagers rubber bands is a recipe for disaster. Even if by accident, a flying rubber band through class makes everyone go from centered and engaged to living on the edge for fear of being hit by the next one. Instead, I hand out plastic stretchy bracelets. They are pliable without being too rubbery, which means no one will ever get shot in the eye with one, which is also a win in your classroom. The list of ideas is virtually endless, but they won't all work for every class. I keep all of my manipulatives in a suitcase in the back of my classroom, and I let students match up their needs with the right one.

Use Lego and Play-Doh. A few years ago, my co-teacher Fians and I had a class that was particularly squirrelly, but we learned that they thrived when they were given an opportunity to learn through creating. While reading *Lord of the Flies,* we noticed that the students were having a hard time remembering which character was which. Our go-to activity when this happens is to have the students create character charts that break each character down. They draw a picture of the character, list character traits, describe how they look, and provide textual evidence to support their claims. For this class, we decided to do something a little bit different. Instead of having them draw a picture of their character, we borrowed some clay from the art room and had the students sculpt their character. When they finished their model, the art teacher fired their creations in the kiln, and we now had little statues of each character. We used what the students made like Dungeons & Dragons figures when explaining what was happening in the story. The only downside was that clay is incredibly messy. It gets everywhere, and makes everyone's hands look like they just strangled Mr. Hankey, the Christmas Poo. Since our first go, we've used Play-Doh instead of clay. It's still fairly inexpensive, and it can be used again and again.

That same year we found that our students were having an especially difficult time with spatial awareness in the same novel. Many students struggled to place where events were happening in the story. Instead of having them draw a map of the island, we had them create scenes from the book with Lego. As luck would have it, Fians still had all of his childhood Lego in his basement. He dusted them off and brought them into class, and for the next two days, we sat around in small groups and built with Lego. Each group created a key scene from the book and then wrote a summary of what they had created. All of the scenes were displayed on the bookshelves on the side of our classroom and were used as references for the remainder of the unit. Both of these projects took extra time, but they allowed us to shake up our class a bit. In both situations, we empowered a number of creative students who usually just sit quietly in class. We had given them the materials to use their imagination and to engage with the story in a whole new way.

It's important to note that not all students loved these projects. Some kids had a hard time creating anything. They wanted to just do the reading and answer questions. That was their strong suit. They had thrived in classes that had them listen to lectures, take notes, and answer comprehension questions. Creative projects made them uncomfortable. Differentiation in the classroom is about both leveling the playing field and requiring students to stretch outside of their comfort zones. Providing a wide variety of activities gives all students opportunities to thrive by doing things that are comfortable for them while they grow by doing things that are *uncomfortable*. The balance of the two is the essence of education.

Use hands-on projects to teach abstract concepts. Every year when our class discusses symbolism, I have the students create a graffiti tag that is a word or an image that says something about who they are. Some kids sketch something out in a font or style that shows how cool or funny they are, while others draw pictures like a crown or basketball to symbolize themselves. After a brief lesson on how to take a regular word or picture and turn it into a proper graffiti tag, we head outside to the front of the school. The kids bring their graffiti mock-ups and create murals on the sidewalk in front of the school with sidewalk chalk. It is a special sight to see teenagers from one of the toughest parts of Philadelphia sitting on the curb making their mark in such a way. Once they start, the small sketches they made in class become much more elaborate and creative. They start blending the chalk colors together and collaborating to create sidewalk chalk graffiti that not only cements into their brains forever what symbolism is but how it exists all around them.

This specific idea clearly works best for an English class, but how can you take what you're teaching in your classroom and make it come alive? In what simple ways can you take an ordinary class and make it extraordinary? This next idea might help you with this.

Transform your classroom. *The Odyssey* is the first book we read at the beginning of every year. To kick it off and create excitement around what my students often consider an old, dusty text, we write ghost stories. Each student is given the job of writing a one-page original ghost story. The kids are told that we will be reading their stories together as a group in class at the end of the week. Now we could just as easily read their often-hilarious tales of horror in our regular classroom, and I'm sure it would be fine, but by sprinkling a little bit of magic on our activity and modifying the classroom a bit, we create a space and a lesson that is far more exciting. When the students walk into class on Friday, they find that I have lowered all of the lights and hung old black torn curtains over the window in the back of the room. I have a YouTube video of a fireplace playing on the projection screen in the front of the room. I play eerie music, and the students take turns reading by battery-powered candlelight in an old chair in the front of the class. This activity wins every year, and it lets students begin to know what they can expect in our classroom. They know that this is no ordinary classroom and that walking through the door to our classroom is like walking through a portal to another dimension. The classroom itself infuses excitement into the students as soon as they walk in. The beauty of this idea is that it can be recreated in any class for any number of lessons. Whether your class is reading Shakespeare or Oliver Jeffers, how might you be able to enhance the experience by simply changing the space in which you are reading? Creating a space for your lesson can be as important as the lesson itself. Ice cream is fine, but how much more exciting is a sundae?

Create a learning culture. I want my students to read a lot. We set aside time every day in class to read. As with most skills in life, if you want students to become better at something, it is important to give them plenty of time to practice. So, every day we read in class. The students sit anywhere they are comfortable: inside a crate, on the couch, on the windowsill, on the floor. Time and space, though, is not enough to make kids good readers. Some students will read whatever you put in front of them. They are good at sitting still and being quiet and doing what they are asked to do. But students are not all created equal, and teaching is not a one-size-fits-all operation. In an effort to create a love of reading in my students and to help them become better readers, I am willing to buy them any book they want, so long as they read. Marine biology, time travel, graphic novels, fantasy, basketball, hip-hop, organized crime . . . You want it, you got it. I have never turned down a book a student has asked for unless it was well below their reading level. This can cost a significant amount of money. To be transparent, I am given money every year from my school to add to my classroom library, but I have friends who have built their classroom libraries by using platforms like DonorsChoose, by writing grants, or by simply hitting up authors and book publishers and asking for books for their classrooms. Our English team is also always on the lookout for one another. Coming into my classroom and finding a pile of books that another teacher found at a library, a yard sale, or thrift store is not uncommon.

But what do you do when your students are resistant to reading or struggle with learning differences like dyslexia or a processing disorder? For those dudes, I try to remove every barrier I can. A few years ago, a friend of mine was getting rid of her old Kindle to get a new one. She asked if anyone would like it, and I raised my hand before she finished her sentence. Devices like this can help kids by allowing them to listen to audiobooks or provide them with text-to-speech assistance when they can't pronounce a word or don't know a definition. I realize a lot of educators disagree about whether students should use devices such as audiobooks to help them read. But reading is power. It literally gives kids the chance to invent themselves, to travel back in time and read other people's minds. It helps them grow as thinkers and find stories that connect to their lives in ways that can leave them changed forever. Therefore, I am willing to do whatever is needed to remove barriers and make reading something they can learn to love.

Education is only ever about the students. We have the power to give students what they need and to help them to grow and learn in ways they never thought possible. Our job as teachers is not simply to transfer knowledge; it is to empower, motivate, and inspire students to grow into their full awesomeness. To achieve this, we need to be examples to our kids. Try ideas, activities, and lessons that put students first. I know this can be a daunting task and that not all of the ideas I've shared can be replicated in your classroom, but it's not about replication. We are DJs. The songs and lessons that move my students might have your students standing awkwardly against the walls. Your job is to find out what interests, learning differences, and so-called limitations your students have and then find the music that makes your class so incredibly awesome that they can't help but engage.

Remember, you can lead a horse to water, but you can't make him drink. But what you can do is make him thirsty. How can you make your students thirsty? It doesn't have to be perfect, and you will have reluctant students with even your best lessons, but keep moving the needle in the right direction and you will find more success and magic in your class than you ever thought possible.

REAL RAP:
REMEMBER WHAT YOUR REAL JOB IS

The main point here is this: classroom management is less about control and more about being clear about why you are doing what you are doing. It's about not expecting kids to "know better." Author and motivational speaker Wayne Dyer once said, "You get treated in life the way you teach people to treat you." Similarly, your students will grow, learn, and behave in your class the way you teach them to. We have one rule in our classroom: Give respect, get respect. I don't expect my students to show me respect merely because I'm the teacher. Legendary teacher Rafe Esquith says that, if he wants his students to be nice and work hard, he will need to be nicer and work harder than all of his students. That is how he sets the bar. If I want my students to show respect to me and their classmates, I need to show them how by being the most respectful one in the room. I set the bar.

Rules, policies, and procedures are just the tip of the iceberg. By building relationships with students, rules become obsolete. I can't overstate this or say it loud enough, building relationships with your students minimizes classroom management issues and increases student engagement. When you show students you truly care by getting to know them, taking an interest in what they care about, and creating wildly engaging lessons, you will find that you don't need to post rules and policies on your classroom walls. Whether it's a simple fix like providing a standing desk or an inexpensive manipulative for a kid or something a little more complicated like incorporating student interests into what you are teaching, allowing students to have a choice in their reading, or just taking the time to make class a bit more exciting, you are showing kids that they matter enough for you to go the distance. My friend Hannah frequently tells students that "love is a verb." As teachers, we can say we care and are invested, or we can show kids that we are.

7

MAKING SOMETHING FROM NOTHING: CLASSROOM DECOR

The Importance of a Welcoming Space

I have loved creating spaces ever since I was a kid. My bedroom always had hidden compartments and impeccable organization. As an adult, I love creating a home that makes people feel welcome from the moment they walk in the door. From the lighting to the smell, I try to create an atmosphere that makes guests feel at home. My tiny garden behind my house is no different. There are secret entrances into my workshop, fairy gardens, tall beautiful flowers, and tons of butterflies. Visitors to our home are often amazed when they walk out our back door into our secret garden. Part of the fun of being a teacher is being able to create a classroom space for my students that does the same thing. A place that makes them feel comfortable and that they want to be in. A place that is inspiring and even feels a bit magical. My classrooms have always been places that

I wanted to be in as well. After all, I'm in my classroom more than my own home, so why wouldn't I put just as much time into it?

One of my favorite classrooms I've ever been invited into was Ms. Howey's middle school English classroom. I met Ms. Howey while giving a talk to her education class at Saint Joseph's University in Philadelphia one evening. After class, I stuck around to speak to her students, and after we talked, she invited me to bring my students to her school to collaborate with her class on a lesson. I picked ten boys, and we drove about twenty minutes outside of the city.

I love taking my students outside of West Philly because it allows them the chance to see how other folks live. It widens their peripheral view and shows what is possible. This particular neighborhood was beautiful. The streets were lined with trees that looked a hundred years old. The homes were not only big but had beautiful gardens around them filled with blooming flowers. This neighborhood was so rich that one house had one of those cute little food pantries in front of it where passersby can grab some free supplies when they are short on funds. I've seen these in a lot of neighborhoods. This one, however, was completely filled with expensive organic products from Whole Foods.

As we arrived at the big, beautiful school, we were guided through the hallways and up to the classroom where the students were waiting for us to arrive. The classroom we walked into looked unlike any classroom I'd ever seen. It looked and felt the way I wish every classroom looked and felt. First, traditional desks had been replaced by an area with beach chairs and a large beach umbrella, a 1950s-style dining room set, a few high-top tables (the kind you'd find in a hipster bar), and standing desks complete with balance boards and wobble boards for kids who had trouble sitting still. The classroom was also decorated in a way that was simultaneously calming and uplifting. Christmas lights hung around the room and colorful painted portraits of students were displayed on the front bulletin board. A chalkboard was painted on one wall across the entire length of the classroom, and here students were encouraged to draw pictures and leave positive messages for one another. It was the best classroom I've ever walked into. Just outside in the hallway, an enormous closet that took up the entire wall was filled with laptops, iPads, and other devices for kids to take at will. No guards. No librarian. Just kids taking equipment as needed to help them learn in ways that best fit them.

Then the craziest thing happened. Ms. Howey brought out cute paper bags filled with an assortment of objects—tape, straws, foil, markers, egg crates, and so on. The students were told to work in groups and to use what was in the bags to create a product that could be sold. They would have thirty minutes to create a product, pinpoint who their buyers would be, and then create either a presentation or a commercial for their product. Ms. Howey instructed the kids to grab their supplies and anything they would need from the giant closet of technology and then *find a place in the school to work on it*. What?! Find a place to work on it? What was that? Where in the world would they go? Isn't anyone watching them? I trust my students, but our school doesn't have a single unused space where I could send them to work on anything. If I want a quiet place to do so much as make a phone call to a kid's parents, I have to go out to my car.

My students immediately shot me a confused look from across the room. They had no idea what to do. They started laughing when they could see I wasn't sure to make of this instruction either. We tried to play it cool, like leaving the room to saunter the hallways and find a random place to work was totally normal. After all of the students grabbed their supplies and left the classroom, I stayed back with the other teachers, but after a few minutes the suspense was too much. I had to see what the students were doing. I went out into the hallway to see where my students had ended up. As I walked around the school, I saw that small niches were built in to the environment here and there to be used as student workspaces. It looked like those little rooms off to the side of a Starbucks that have the cozy little tables and chairs for folks to "work from home." It was awesome. There were big, beautiful windows stretching from floor to ceiling, cozy chairs with coffee tables, bean bag chairs . . . Like I said before, it looked and felt the way school should look and feel. Ms. Howey's classroom and school made kids want to show up and engage.

Making Something from Nothing

A quick search on Pinterest or any of your favorite social media platforms can leave teachers with limited means, little experience, or a ton of restrictive school policies feeling jealous. Maybe you don't have the space, the money, or the materials. Unfortunately, no amount of jealousy or wishing will get your students a school like this. If you're feeling like that, however, I have good news for you: As I walked around the hallways that day looking for my students, I peeked into a number of other classrooms. Many looked no more impressive than any other classrooms I've been in. It turned out Ms. Howey's classroom wasn't special just because she had money for supplies and decorations. It was special because she was willing to give her time and energy to make the room into a place that was incredible for her students. No matter what their school is like, teachers seem to have a superpower to *make something from nothing.* Just like the amazing drummer making money as a street performer by banging on buckets, the graffiti artist making the wall his canvas, or that friend making a dress or jacket from the thrift store look like a million dollars, teachers learn to make places of wonder and awe with little to no budget. You can do the same thing. I have managed to make a classroom for my students that I love walking into every day.

Before I talk about how I did it, I want to say on the front end that I know schools have a lot of rules about what you can and can't do in the classroom. Some of you reading this aren't allowed to put holes in your walls, paint your classrooms, use tape, or bring unauthorized furniture into school spaces. Some of you don't even *have* classrooms. I get it. Really. But what are you going to do about it?

Don't have a classroom? Ask for a closet or a wall. Got stuck being the teacher with the cart? Make it the greatest teacher cart that ever rolled down your school's hallways! Grab some battery-powered lights, a boom box, and a bubble machine, and make it a party wherever you go.

My first classroom that was strictly my own in West Philadelphia was a challenge. The previous year I was told that I would be getting my own room for the following school year. When I came back that August, I was given the keys to a room that looked like a regular-sized classroom had a baby. It was a little, tiny, baby room.

I've had every kind of classroom over the years. I've taught in a trailer; a basement; a windowless, leaky room in an old factory; a shared room. This time I was given a room that was so small I couldn't fit a teacher desk in there, and I could only make rows of desks that went four deep. It was so bad it was hilarious. I could have gotten pissed, but instead I decided to make this tiny room the greatest classroom ever. Since it was so small, no one else was scheduled to use it, which gave me the freedom to make it look however I wanted it to look.

If you teach high school, you know that teacher supply stores don't have much to offer for secondary school classrooms. The cooler posters that do exist on "teacher-y" websites are expensive. And honestly what kid has ever learned something from a poster in a teacher's room? You're supposed to be paying attention or working diligently in class, not looking all over the place and reading about similes and metaphors on the far side of the classroom. So, instead of ordering a bunch of weird expensive crap from the store, I decided to make my own weird inexpensive crap. Before transforming my tiny classroom, I did a quick check in with my main man Mr. Pascal, the high school dean, and asked if he thought I could get away with using blackboard paint on the walls in my room. As soon as he gave me the green light, I got some blackboard paint and painted a black stripe about three feet wide across the entire front wall of the classroom.

Side note: Blackboard paint is expensive, and they only sell it in quart-sized cans. You can get a gallon of black paint way cheaper and have paint to spare. Side side note: I know not everyone can paint their walls, but you could achieve the same effect by painting pieces of plywood that you could temporarily hang on your walls or using chalkboard contact paper.

My next step was to find artwork online for each of the books we were going to read that year. In lieu of spending money on expensive posters, I planned on making my own artwork to showcase the books. I hooked a projector up to my computer and projected the images onto the wall. I traced them with a pencil, and then used chalk to make the final picture. For the cost of a can of paint (the cheap stuff at that) and a box of chalk, I was able to make artwork on my classroom walls that was unlike anything in any other classroom.

That year my department head also informed us that we would each be given one hundred dollars to spend on a bookshelf for our rooms. Our school didn't have room for a library, so instead we would receive money each year to buy independent reading books for our classrooms. When I got my gift card to buy my shelves, I opted instead to go to Home Depot and buy a sheet of MDF and some stainless-steel L brackets. MDF is similar to plywood but much cheaper. You can get a sheet for about twenty-six dollars.

I used the MDF to make very simple "floating" bookshelves for my classroom walls. It would have been way easier to run to IKEA and grab bookshelves, but I wanted my room to look unusual and inspiring, so I took the extra time to build the shelves. I have a video on my YouTube channel showing exactly how I made these shelves and the supplies I used. They are so simple that, if you know how to saw a board and drive a screw, you can whip some up in no time. When they were ready, I loaded them in the car and did a late-night run to my school to install them. To create the illusion that they were floating, I would have to screw the shelves into the wall using wall anchors. This meant I had to make a *lot* of holes in the wall to ensure the shelves would stay up. This would be one of those times when I asked for forgiveness instead of permission. If the shelves turned out the way I hoped they would, it would look awesome, and I knew I wouldn't get in trouble. If they didn't, well, that would be a problem I would have to handle when it happened. The bottom line is that the things I create are all about the students, so I'm willing to try ideas that might get me in a little trouble. If this project had only been about me and how cool my room could look, that would be a different story.

With the help of my sisters-in-law, Kayla and Klara, and my wife, Jenni, we painted and hung all of the shelves in one night. We were at school until four in the morning, but the shelves turned out better than I could have hoped. For the cost of a bookshelf at any big box store, I was able to build simple custom bookshelves that made kids want to look at the books.

Side note: If you are trusted enough to be in your school after hours, it is literally *the best*. I bring snacks and turn the volume on the music all the way up, and no one is around to be bothered or to disrupt you. Some of my favorite moments have been hanging at school after hours. Even my own kids love it. Brody and Marley have been visiting my school since they were toddlers. When they go with me, they ride their Big Wheels, skateboards, and scooters around the hallways, play with the skeletons in the science lab, or watch movies and play video games on the interactive screen in my classroom.

The following night I went back to the school and hung "flying books" from my classroom ceiling. I made them out of old books my local library was giving away. The simplest versions of these books are made by simply screwing an eye hook into the spine of a book and then suspending the book from the ceiling with clear fishing line to create the illusion that they are flying. I get a lot of questions from my YouTube viewers about "ruining" books for aesthetic purposes.

Rest assured, book lovers, the books I use are either in a language other than English or are about a topic or by an author I have decided no one has any interest in. For example, two of the books currently hanging from my ceiling are Kato Kaelin's autobiography and a book from the 1960s on how to tan animal hides. I felt like these were pretty safe bets. If you are into DIY animal skin drying or dollar store autobiographies about the guy who was living in OJ's pool house in 1994, I apologize.

Of all the fun details I applied to my room that year, my favorite by far was the teacher office I created. As I mentioned, the room was too small for a traditional teacher desk. Although I didn't need a desk for grading papers, I did need a place to keep my supplies and confidential paperwork. I thought about making a murphy bed–style desk or a bunk desk that would sit above the students' desks, but both of them seemed a bit dangerous. Now I'm not afraid of danger, but my children have to eat, so I went for a safer option this time. The idea started with cleaning out a closet that sat in the front corner of the classroom. It was filled to the brim with boxes of old tests and papers that I'm sure no one even knew were there. Again, I went to school after hours, found a hand truck, and hauled about forty boxes of random papers to the basement of the school, adding it to another nest of papers at least as large in an even bigger closet. This was almost ten years ago, and to my knowledge, no one has ever gone looking for these documents.

The next step was to make a desk. School basements are often the dumping grounds for all of the crap teachers have discarded over the years. It is where I have found some of my favorite treasures. If you ever have a spare moment, consider moseying down to your school's basement to see what you can find. On this particular trip, I found an eight-foot-long piece of laminate countertop. Half of it had rotted away from the water that drips into the basement, but the other half was salvageable. I cut off the three feet that I needed and discarded the rest. I now had a smooth, custom-fitted desk top for my closet office. Over the next few days I installed shelving, a pencil sharpener, and under-shelf lighting that I picked up from IKEA for only a few bucks; hung pictures on the wall; and decorated with a dead plant. I knew a plant could never survive in there without sunlight, but the idea of having a dead plant in my "office" seemed perfectly ironic and hilarious. To finish it off, I bought a "store hours" sign from an office supply store. I filled out my available office hours and hung it on the closet door. It was awesome. I went from no room for a desk to the most ludicrously awesome desk in the school.

The lesson here is that schools and teachers are often under-funded and don't have enough room, but there's always a way to make things at least a little bit more awesome. I realize that I got away with things that some of you would not get away with in your own school. I don't have an answer for every problem, but I hope my experiences encourage you to believe in your own creativity. You can find a solution to almost any classroom issue you might face by thinking creatively.

One of my favorite TED Talks of all time and one that I show my students every year is the presentation by Phil Hansen. Phil is an artist whose passion was pointillism, a particular type of drawing or painting in which the artist creates a picture using thousands of dots. From up close, the piece looks like a series of random dots, but from a bit of a distance, the picture takes on a life and a shape. Phil had spent years perfecting his craft, but as he grew in his ability, he noticed his hand began to shake uncontrollably. Over time, the shaking got worse until he gave up and left art completely. A year later, he couldn't stand it any longer and decided to see a doctor. The doctor told him that the tremor was the result of the thousands, if not millions, of dots Phil had made in an effort to create his art. The only answer was for him to stop making the style of art he loved. If he continued, the shaking would get only get worse. Phil asked the doctor point blank what he should do, and the doctor's answer was, "Why not embrace the shake?" Not knowing what else to do and feeling like his career was already over, Phil took a chance and followed the doctor's advice. He started creating pictures out of squiggly lines. The same basic principles of pointillism were intact; Phil had merely replaced the dots with squiggles. From these drawings, Phil got the idea of creating larger, more ambitious creations, like a wall-sized portrait of Bruce Lee he made by karate chopping paint onto his canvas or the enormous re-creation of the Mona Lisa he made using only the grease from a ton of McDonald's hamburgers. Phil discovered that his greatest creativity lay in finding ways to beat limitation, and that can be the same for all of us.

What I'm getting at here is that you have that same ability to "embrace the shake." Your "shake" might not be the same as Phil's, but that's because our so-called limitations truly do make us unique. Maybe your school doesn't allow you to paint on your walls. Maybe you don't even have walls. My friend Ms. May from the YouTube channel *One Fab Teacher* doesn't have walls that go to the ceiling in her classroom. She doesn't even have doors! All of the classroom spaces are separated by partitions that are about six to seven feet tall, and the doors have been replaced with curtains. It's like teaching in cubicles. The question isn't, "What is your limitation?" The question is, "What are you going to do with it?"

A Tour of My Current Classroom

My current classroom is one of my favorite spaces I've ever created. It literally makes me happy every time I walk into it. That is no accident. Though my room can look large when seen on YouTube and Instagram, it's actually pretty small and is a weird L shape. About a quarter of my classroom is cut off because the elevator creates a large bump-out in the floor plan. As I said before, I'm in my classroom between eight and twelve hours a day, which is more waking hours than I'm in my own home, so making a space that inspires me is critical to my ability to be the best teacher I can be. When

I began creating this room, I stayed away from teacher stores and online school supply outlets; instead I started collecting images of creative and inspiring studios that I loved—like the art studios of stuff maker Mac Premo and picture book creator Oliver Jeffers. I also looked at the maker space of the famous inventor Thomas Edison and YouTuber Casey Neistat. I wanted my room to invoke a sense of wonder and fun but still be a well-organized environment that would allow the students to learn in ways that fit their needs.

Before I took it over, my current room had been a tiny school library. Due to a lack of space in the school, it was also used periodically for classes that were presided over by a series of incredibly sloppy teachers. It was a dismal place. Cheap, white laminate bookshelves loaded with books that no student would ever read lined every wall. The front wall was an awful yellowish-brown color that resembled old mustard or baby poop. Trash was everywhere—behind books, in drawers, under desks. The teacher's desk was a giant L-shaped monster with pieces falling off and drawers so jacked they wouldn't open. The rest of the room was filled with a wild array of furniture that had no foreseeable use—podiums shoved in the corner, filing cabinets filled with junk, end tables that were like display stands for papers completed years ago.

After my success in transforming my little baby room across the hall, I was excited to have a bigger classroom in which to create a learning space. I didn't know yet if I would have a roommate and what ideas they might have. Some of the classrooms in my school made you sad when you walked into them, and I was nervous about potentially sharing a room with someone who might try to make the room look like Eeyore felt. I decided to start working on the space as if it were my own. I hoped that whoever ended up rooming with me would be so impressed they would just go with my flow and not add anything. I also decided to go full tilt on this new room, asking for forgiveness instead of permission. I hoped that if I did all of this work in August, just before the staff came back to school, I would amaze teachers and administrators alike, and they would be so over-whelmed by the beauty of it all they wouldn't think about the paint color or how many holes I had put in the walls.

To see my classroom with your own eyes, you can visit my YouTube channel, *Real Rap with Reynolds*, but I'll give you a quick text-based tour right here. Our classroom, just like in my tiny baby room, has a thick black line of paint that stretches all the way around the top of the room. On the front wall, I've drawn scenes from all of the books we read in class. This year that line up was *The Odyssey, Of Mice and Men, Persepolis, The Merchant of Venice,* and *Lord of the Flies.* One of the best things about drawing on your walls is that you can use any image you find online. It doesn't necessarily need to be the cover of the book. For Shakespeare, I found a cool image from the cover of a playbill. For *Persepolis,* I drew one of my favorite images from the graphic novel. The picture for *The Odyssey* is one of Odysseus and the Cyclops facing off that looks like a drawing from a manga comic. On one of the side walls, I painted the outline of a huge boombox with the words "Make Something from Nothing" above it. This is one of the mottoes of our classroom because I want my students to be excited about limitations. They make us up our game and become more creative. The wall next to that has simple plywood ledges on which I display independent reading books. I know fortune cookies have told us not to judge a book by its cover, but have you seen the covers that are on young adult books these days? They are works of art. They are made to be fallen in love with. So, why not create a simple space to display them so a kid might pick one up?

Halfway down my classroom wall, I have a series of posters I framed with cheap IKEA frames. These are all books that changed my life: *On the Road, Into the Wild, Batman,* and *My Side of the Mountain.* By proudly displaying the covers of the books that have meant something to me like they are trophies, I convey to my students how important books have been in my life. This simple act opens opportunities to talk with students about why reading is important and how books can help to challenge your thinking and allow you to live your best possible life. No matter what class you teach, you can hang your own inspiration on the walls. Don't feel limited by your subject matter. Who's your favorite scientist, mathematician, or musician? Honor them and strike up a conversation with your students by simply hanging a framed picture or poster of them on the wall. For me, it's important that the images are framed. I've had many posters over the years that I've hung up repeatedly, and every year they get a little more creased and tattered after being stored for the summer in my attic, and the corners accumulate more and more holes from reapplying thumbtacks each year. I'm a grown man, not a college student. I want my classroom aesthetic to reflect that. I don't want a classroom that looks like a dorm room or some kid's first apartment. When you get your first place, everyone wants to give you all their old crap so they can feel like they helped, but really they're just getting rid of all of the stuff in their garage that they can't bring themselves to put on the curb. You end up with a brand-new crib filled with Grandma's lamps from when she first got married, Aunt Kath's end tables and desk that she put in the basement after she went through her country stage, Pop's macramé table that he picked up when he was stationed on the west coast in '74, and a handsome rug your mom passed on to you so she can parlay her act of kindness into a new rug. Instead of the dope new apartment you envisioned, the one that would make you the envy of everyone who entered, you now have the makings of a thrift store.

Teachers are the same way. They're very happy to give you all of the old crap they've been hoarding since the beginning of their career. Half of it was probably given to them by someone else when they started out. You'll be offered rolls of faded bulletin board paper in colors you don't even like, a periodic table poster that's so old it might be missing a few elements, bookshelves that you have to secure to the wall because they might take a kid out if they stand free.

Don't fall for that! Like Ms. Howey's classroom, your classroom, closet, cart, or corner should be the envy of the school. It should make you stoked every time you see it, and it should make kids *want* to be in your room or partying in the hallway as your cart rolls by. I love building new stuff and making upgrades for my classroom every year.

Since that first year in my new room, I've added a couch and chair that were props from the school play, a nine-foot tree I made of driftwood from the Delaware River, and even more flying books, floating bookshelves, and standing desks. I love little hidden surprises that light people up when they discover them, so I placed cheap, battery-powered motion-activated lights in the lockers under the teacher desk in front of my room. I keep certain supplies in the lockers so I don't have to walk through the students to the back of the room over and over. When someone opens the door, they're always surprised to find that it lights up automatically, making everything easy to find. I also keep all of the remote controls for the smartboard and projector in old books that look ordinary but have a secret compartment carved out of them. All of the cheap unsightly white laminate shelves have been reorganized, and I covered them with new wooden fronts to give the illusion that they are far more expensive and custom than they actually are. This new wooden ledge also allowed me to place light strips under each shelf, making my bookshelves look more attractive to potential readers. My room is completely customized and contains everything I might possibly need for a project or assignment. This concept came from the American inventor Thomas Edison. In his Menlo Park laboratory, Edison liked to keep "a stock of almost every conceivable material." He was known for having everything from hooves to human hair in stock to avoid any delay in his creations. Although I've opted out of keeping human hair and hooves in supply, I do try to have on hand every conceivable item that might be useful to my students and the school's staff— screws, tools, poster board, foam core board, spray paint, stencils, extra pairs of reading glasses for forgetful students, highlighters, and much more, all organized and labeled in their own bin, locker, or drawer for quick and easy access.

 ## REAL RAP:

STUDENTS NEED INSPIRING SPACES

If we want students to be inspired, creative, happy, and productive, we need to create classrooms that reflect those aspirations. If your room has the same plain white walls and fluorescent lights as a hospital room, if trash accumulates on the floor and the walls are grimy, what message are we sending our students? How can we expect our kids to go above and beyond, when we do not? Classrooms should inspire magic and creativity. They should make students want to come to class and engage. You don't need a lot of money to do this. Look online for creative alternatives to what expensive stores want to sell you. Search Craigslist and Facebook Marketplace for secondhand tables, chairs, or bookshelves that can make your room a comfortable spot for learning. Create art on your walls, write on the desks, and think outside the box to fashion the classroom you've always wanted to teach in. If your school has rules against hanging things on the walls or having unauthorized furniture in the classrooms, try to "embrace the shake," like Phil Hansen. If your school doesn't have money to create a warm and welcoming space for students, consider making something from nothing. Look around at what you do have, and see how you can make it work. You are not alone. Thousands of teachers and creators have found success when faced with the same problems you are now facing. Seek them out, and copy their ideas. Motivational author and speaker Tony Robbins says that "success leaves clues." Look for the clues left by those who have already figured out the answer to your classroom decor problems. In doing this, you will make a classroom that not only inspires you and your students but also serves as a peaceful and refreshing space for staff to visit. A creative and fun classroom is a gift to everyone who walks through your door.

8

TOXIC TEACHERS AND SELF-CARE

Dealing with Toxicity

One of the issues that completely blindsided me when I began teaching was dealing with what I call toxic teachers. These are the teachers whose attitudes and behaviors permeate school culture like a fart. They say your lessons are too much, the way you high five every kid in the hallway is over the top, the magical classroom decor you have created is unnecessary, your out-of-the-box thinking on lessons, organization, parent connections, and class trips is too excessive. Worst of all, they berate the students behind their backs. Their toxicity permeates their classrooms and lessons, making school unbearable for the children they claim to educate. Like the walking dead, they trudge around the school spreading their funk and bad attitudes. They love Friday and hate Monday. They fill the teachers' lounge with trash talk and complain about anything and everything.

On the front end, I want to say that I am not immune to this. I have talked my fair share of trash over the years. I have weeks when I cannot wait for the last bell on Friday. I've complained, been jealous, been rude, and dogged students and teachers in the staff lounge. I am no better than any other teacher. Having said that, I also don't think these behaviors are binary. I have never met a teacher who is either nice or mean, strictly positive or negative, good or bad. We are all a mix of both. We are all masterpieces in progress. The bigger question is how do we, as teachers and administrators, move the needle in our schools away from gloomy, jealous, and bitter and in the direction of fun, uplifting, and exciting? I know how daunting this task can feel, especially if you feel like you are the only one in your school who loves their job. Or maybe you have slipped into being the apathetic teacher, and you don't want to be that anymore. Either way, I want to remind you that you are more powerful than you think. Changing your school's toxic culture comes down to making the choice to do so. You probably can't change everything, but you can change something, and then change something else, and then another thing! The best part is that you can do it a thousand different ways. The transformation from toxic to awesome can be as simple as a series of small changes.

From Defense to Offense

One of the biggest changes I've made in my life to help me have the best days I can is switching my mindset from defense to offense. I used to wake up with enough time in my morning to shower, get dressed, and down a cup of coffee. I would then drive to school with just enough time to get my room ready for the day before the first bell would ring. This schedule left me no room for error. If my wife needed me to do something before leaving the house or I hit traffic, I was instantly running late and overwhelmed with anxiety. In my experience, the worst way to arrive at school is feeling rushed or flustered. It makes my interactions with my students and coworkers awkward and unkind and doesn't help me start the day on the right foot.

The switch I made was to get up earlier. I know how unattractive this sounds, but give it a try for a while. I guarantee that it will change your life. I wake up an hour before I need to, at four forty-five, to go through the same exact series of events every morning. By keeping it exactly the same every day, I don't have to think about anything. It's second nature. My morning routine looks like this.

Wake up. As soon as my alarm goes off, I immediately get up, walk downstairs, and sit in the large armchair in my living room.

For ten minutes, I meditate and clear my mind. I let all of my thoughts go and just focus on my breathing. I don't want my thoughts happening to me. I am in control.

For five minutes, I think of all that I am grateful for. I start small and think about the fact that I have a chair to sit in or that my house has heating or air conditioning. I then think of how happy I am for my family and my life. I also think about people who drive me crazy or have brought me a lot of stress in my life. I force myself to think of something about them that I can be grateful for. If I'm having a hard time with a particular teacher or student, I make myself think of at least one positive attribute that they have. Maybe it's a teacher who is rude to you every day or talks about you behind your back, but you do know that they willingly attend every football game to support the students. Maybe the kid who is driving you to drink shares his lunch with someone who needs it every day. By doing this, you are disrupting your thought pattern. You are not letting your mind and feelings run wild. You are in charge.

For ten minutes, I pray. Some days, this means I simply sit in silence and listen. Some days, I pray for particular people and situations. Other days, I just talk about what I'm feeling or thinking. It's not about doing it a specific way. It's about connection with and surrender to something larger than myself.

For fifteen minutes, I read something that will further the mindset I want to cultivate. This is no time for your favorite murder mystery. I want to put myself in a place of gratitude and wonder. If left to its own devices, upon waking, my head goes immediately to the to-do list, what bills I need to pay, how I could be a better dad, or any other number of self-deprecating thoughts. You'll find a more extensive list in the appendix, but some of my very favorite books for my morning reading are *I Feel Great and You Will Too* by Pat Croce, *Tattoos on the Heart* by Father Gregory Boyle, and *The World According to Mister Rogers*. These books fill me with hope and help me get excited about the day. That is exactly how I want to start my day, filled with hope—hope that I can be of service, that I can remain playful, that I can have the courage to step outside of my comfort zone and be the best teacher and colleague I can be.

For twenty minutes, I sit with my wife, Jenni, and have coffee. This is my favorite part of my morning and one of my favorite parts of my day. We call it our morning meeting. In this time, we talk about our life dreams. Whether it's the farm we want to own or the life we want for our kids, we use this time to not only talk about what we want but exactly how we will get there. This is a sacred time that we share. It is like a gift we give to each other at the start of each day.

For the thirty minutes I'm commuting to work, I listen to a podcast or music that will fill me with some sort of goodness. I listen to many different podcasts, and I've listed some of my favorites in the appendix, but regardless of which one I choose on a given day, I stick with episodes that are about something positive in nature. I want to step out of my car in the school parking lot overwhelmed with goodness. Happiness is contagious, and I want to spread it around as much as I can. For me, the only way this can happen is by constantly filling myself up with all the goodness I can.

I'm no professional at any of this stuff. I just know that getting up early and running through these steps makes me feel great in the morning, and when I feel great, I am far better equipped to handle whatever the day brings—the copier in the office running out of paper, my students being late, a rude comment from another teacher, a fire drill in the middle of my perfect classroom activity. All of the same stuff happens; I just feel like I have options in how I choose to deal with it.

Whenever I meet people who have watched me on YouTube or seen me at a speaking engagement, they often comment about how positive I am. They're right; I am positive and optimistic for the most part, but the misconception is that this comes easily to me. In fact, this is not at all how I am naturally wired. I am sad a lot. I'd say that the majority of my thirties was spent in darkness. I often feel alone at holidays, and I long for my parents to be alive again. I feel like I'm not as good of a father or husband as I should be. I'm not good enough as a teacher or friend, and any day now, people are going to figure this out, and I will be left alone again. Teaching is an incredibly taxing profession. The paperwork, the grading, the preparation, the discipline issues, and the effort to help students, parents, and colleagues are beyond exhausting. All of this can leave you feeling like you are a failure who never should have taken this path to begin with. I want you to know that I feel these things too—all of them. For this reason, I work hard to forge the state of mind I want. I know this is a book about teaching, but don't get it twisted, mindset is everything in this job. You need to make sure that your mental and physical health is at the top of your priority list. Before I share with you some of my ideas and practices I use to stay at the top of my game, I want to say that this, too, isn't easy for me. I hate exercise, green juice is terrible and tastes like sadness, and I really love beer and bread. I do the things I do because I want a life that is unbelievably awesome, and I want to share that awesomeness with everyone I meet. Henry David Thoreau wrote, "The mass of men live lives of quiet desperation." I've been there in the dark and the sadness, but I've also tasted what it's like to live out loud, to experience magic and wonder, and to be filled with love. Both experiences require a lot from you, but I prefer the latter. Here are some ways I keep my mental and physical health at its best.

Play music everywhere. No matter where I am, I have music on, the louder the better. I want to fill my house, my shed, my classroom, and my car with music. Music makes me want to dance, to run harder, to give a high five, and to spread the love. The power of music is undeniable. I could be driving my car, stuck in traffic, pissed that I'm running late for an appointment, but then just the right song comes on, and I am helpless to its power. I can't help but sing along and play the drums on my steering wheel.

Go on retreats. Ideally, I try to go on a silent retreat four times a year. A great place just outside of Philadelphia offers one-room hermitages where I can step away from my everyday life and sit in silence with myself. I'll bring books and a journal, but no technology, not even music. Blaise Pascal said, "All men's miseries derive from not being able to sit in a quiet room alone," and Leonardo da Vinci said, "Every now and then go away, have a little relaxation, for when you come back to your work your judgment will be surer; since to remain constantly at work will cause you to lose power of judgement . . . Go some distance away because the work appears smaller and more of it can be taken in at a glance, and a lack of harmony or proportion is more readily seen." These quotes are two I think of every time I go on retreat. My life in the classroom is so wonderfully and terribly wild that I need to step away and sit in silence. No phone. No computer. No television. No home projects. Just me. In doing this, you begin to see that the stressful things in your life aren't as big as you thought. Standing in the middle of a hurricane is terrifying. You can't see what's happening or which way to go to find help. From space, a hurricane looks far less terrifying. Once in a while, consider finding a small, quiet place where you can retreat and find peace so you can return to your life in the classroom with a tranquil heart.

Do stuff that sucks on purpose. As I write this, I am in the middle of a challenge I set for myself to run a mile every day for a year—no days off for any reason. Christmas morning, the day my beloved grandmother passed away, the day my father-in-law passed away, the nights after I drink a little too much, in the rain, snow, and hail, after the longest, hardest days at school, jet-lagged, I run. Last year was a terribly difficult year in our school. A lot of students I deeply care for needed a lot of assistance. Teachers were struggling. Our family was going through financial difficulties, and our kids' school was making it very clear that they were not willing to do what was needed to help our children. I felt completely overwhelmed and run down. Early one morning, I was reading David Goggins's book *You Can't Hurt Me* when I was struck powerfully by these words: "When your mind is telling you you're done, you're really only 40 percent done." Something about this idea moved me to want to go on offense instead of defense. I was having my ass kicked by life, so I thought, what would happen if I deliberately increased my own stress? If I put *myself* in difficult mental and physical situations, I gain power over my stress, thereby taking the power away from my external stressors. In short, I would kick my own ass before someone else could do it for me. I found that by self-inducing a little bit of suffering, the stressors in my life seemed far less potent. I began running every day. The minimum was a mile, and the cap was five miles. I also began attending hot yoga classes once or twice a week. If you want the rest of your day to feel like a walk in the park, try sweating yourself into a puddle in a hot yoga class for an hour. To be clear, I'm not advocating that you not take a break or lessen your workload; I just think it's important to take control of where your stress comes from. Goggins says in his book, "Doing things—even small things—that make you uncomfortable will help make you strong."

Make time for love. My wife and I actually schedule date nights right on our kitchen calendar. If I don't make a point of scheduling it, I will keep my head down and work all the time. If it's on the schedule, I make it a priority. Whether it's stepping out for beers, seeing a movie, or just driving around our neighborhood eating french fries and milkshakes, date nights are on the schedule.

Make time for the kids. Just as I schedule time with my wife, I do the same thing with my kids. Sometimes it's just a night in together watching a movie or playing video games; other times it's heading out to the woods or the beach. During the time with my wife and kids, I don't touch my phone unless it's absolutely necessary. I don't talk about work or anything stressful. This is time for fun.

Know when to close up shop. Every night I set a time when I know I need to be finished with my work for the day. I make a promise to myself that I will not work past that time. Sometimes I need to get a lot done, so I might work late into the night to meet a deadline, but even then, my hard out might be midnight or one in the morning. Other days I might want to get up early and finish my work by nine in the morning. Either way I like to keep my promises, so no matter what's happening, I quit at the agreed time. This allows me to keep from working feverishly into the night until I fall asleep at my desk. It also gives me a finish line. In any race, it's easier to push yourself and focus when you know where the finish line is.

Eat lunch with students and colleagues. I love eating lunch with my students. It is a time to just talk with them and find out who they are as people. It also gives them a chance to get to know me as a person. Similarly, eating with a group of fun-loving and positive teachers can be life-giving. Lunch always takes place in my classroom with the lights low to change the vibe of the classroom. One of my favorite things our group has done this year is Comedian Friday. I have a large number of students who are into stand-up comedy, so every Friday we watch a different comedian and break down their set. We look at things like, how did they open their set? How long did they hold their pause to get an extra laugh out of the audience? How important was their word choice in a particular joke? It's a blast! We laugh our faces off and learn a little something and then go back to class filled with joy.

Eat right. When I started teaching, I ate the same way I did when I was in the fifth grade. I would eat waffles for breakfast. For lunch, I would have a peanut butter and jelly sandwich, cookies, and an enormous amount of iced tea. I didn't know it at the time, but this diet made me sluggish and unmotivated to teach. These days, my diet is aimed at helping me have the most energy I possibly can. I drink a small cup of coffee with a little cream in the morning and try not to eat until one in the afternoon as part of my intermittent fasting regimen. For lunch, I either eat a salad and a protein bar or I drink this awful green juice that my wife makes for me. The juice tastes like sadness, but it gives me the boost I need to bring my A game to my afternoon classes. The important thing here is to not get hung up on the details. It's about finding food that doesn't just fill your belly but makes your body feel great and ready for action.

Sleep. I don't like to sleep. It always feels like a waste of time. However, I know it's important for a million different reasons. In an effort to maximize the quality of the sleep that I do get, my wife and I made a few changes to our sleep routine. A couple of years ago, we bought a new mattress. I don't know why it was such a surprise to either of us, but a brand-new mattress made a huge difference in the quality of sleep we got each night. We also bought blackout curtains and removed all of the tiny lights from our bedroom. Once we put up our new blackout curtains, it was hilarious to us to see all of the tiny little lights that existed in our room. The lights on the television, the printer, the laptop, and the phone charger suddenly felt like little laser beams shooting us in the eye when we tried to sleep. We covered all of the lights with black electrical tape, and I can't tell you how much darker and more peaceful our room became. The last change we made was to begin taking CBD oil before we slept. This has made the biggest difference of all. The first night I took CBD oil, I slept better than I had in ten years. It was truly amazing to wake up feeling completely refreshed and excited about the day.

Reverse-engineer your life. Where I am going in life is no mystery. I know exactly where I want to live, what truck I want to own, what guests I want to have visit my classroom, and where I want to go on vacation. A few years ago, my wife and I began taking the time to dream about the life we wanted. We didn't dream small, either. The exercise we created demanded that we think as big as possible. It was an amazing activity because it allowed us to see what our ideal life would look like. We then priced out that ideal life, and it turned out that our incredible ideal lifestyle cost a fraction of what we thought it would cost! That dream went from completely unattainable to something we could actually plan out and achieve. After doing this for our personal life, I began dreaming about my school life. I began asking myself what school would look like if it was the greatest—no restrictions. I began to dream about what kind of classroom space I would like to teach in, who I'd like to have visit us, where I would take my students to visit and explore, and how my colleagues and I could have the most amazing and creative lessons and activities together. I think a lot of us approach lesson planning with the rules, policies, and procedures in mind. It's hard to be creative when you're preoccupied with what you're not allowed to do. Dare to shake off the shackles and dream big for you and your students! Once you hatch the idea and make the plan to bring it to fruition, you might be surprised that your dreams are actually much closer to reality than you thought.

Like my friend told me, if there's no gas in the car, no one's going anywhere. The most important part of staying mentally and physically strong is to remember that you have to take care of yourself or you won't be able to take care of anyone else. It's like on an airplane when they tell you to use the oxygen mask yourself before you try to help anyone else. You can't help anyone if you've passed out from lack of oxygen, and you can't give your students what you don't have in yourself. Be kind to yourself and give yourself some love.

Making Your Own Party

Another change I've made is I no longer wait to be invited to someone else's party; I make my own party. If I have my own party, I decide who is invited. I am not obligated to have people around who are glooming up my scene. Instead of eating in the teachers' lounge, I eat in my classroom or on the steps outside of the school. I invite people to eat with me who I think are fun or who motivate me. When you hang out in the teachers' lounge, you often walk into a conversation that is already in progress, and you have two choices: join in or sit quietly. Joining in sounds great if everyone is talking about something you enjoy, but if not, it can be a drag to sit and listen to teachers complain again and again about your administration or how the kids are driving them nuts. In my classroom, we sit together and laugh and tell stories and share experiences. The best part is that if one of our crew is having a difficult day, they have people who care about them right there. We can offer advice or just sit with them in their time of need.

What do you do when the weeks have been long for everyone and the whole school is running low on enchantment? Remind your community that they are appreciated. Mark Twain once said, "I can live for two months on a good compliment." Not to dog Mr. Twain, but two months might be a bit of a stretch. However, a good compliment from an unexpected source can definitely brighten your day. One of my friends at school, Ms. Lewis, often has students write quick notes to teachers who they think are fantastic in some way. Maybe they're thankful for the extra help the teacher always gives or perhaps there's a certain lesson that they loved. Maybe they appreciate that the teacher always makes them feel seen or that they have a way of making class fun. After the kids write the notes, she makes stacks of each teacher's notes and either places them in the teacher's mailbox or has the students deliver them. Few things can make your day better than getting a grateful note from a kid who you didn't think even liked you or a kid who you didn't think cared about anything. Every time Ms. Lewis does this, it completely changes the vibe of my classroom because it's a boost to my morale. The awesome part is that she doesn't have to do anything but give the kids time and space to be kind.

One of the best things you can do when you're feeling stressed and overwhelmed at school is to put yourself near people who are vibrating on a higher level than you are. I realize that sounds like a very hippy-dippy, I-make-my-own-maple-syrup-and-wear-Birkenstocks kind of thing to say, but that's just how it is. Also, my apologies to all the folks out there wearing Birkenstocks while they enjoy their homemade sugary goodness. I do not mean to offend.

In my last year teaching in Camden, the ninth-grade team was moved out of the high school building and into the top floor of the middle school. The idea, we were told by administration, was to keep the ninth graders away from the upperclassmen. This was the same idea as when our school moved our team into a series of trailers behind the school building one year. The school was concerned that they would have more discipline issues with the incoming freshmen if they saw how the upperclassmen acted. In this upper hallway, we were closed off from the rest of the school. The students could only leave the floor if they were being escorted to the lunchroom or the gym by a teacher. Likewise, the teachers were cut off from the rest of the faculty. Everyone else we knew was on the far side of the school in a different building, so it was rare for us to see our friends. In some ways, it felt like we were all being punished by being exiled. In retrospect, however, this ended up being one of my favorite years I've ever had in the classroom and one of my favorite teams I have ever worked with.

As it turned out, we were far enough away from the high school that you were more likely to see a yeti walk down the hallway than to see an administrator. Our students also had schedules that split their time upstairs into two parts. They would have classes with us in the morning and then be taken to lunch and gym in the main high school building. This left the staff with a sixty to ninety minutes of uninterrupted time together in our maiden's tower. It proved to be one of the greatest schedules of all time. We had time to plan and co-plan, time to talk and figure out how to help students, time to see what the other teachers were doing in class that day and to bounce new ideas off one another. More than anything, we had fun together. Nothing helps you deal with a toxic school environment like laughing. That year, we made sure everything was fun. When Thanksgiving came around, we decided to have a Thanksgiving-style lunch together in our tiny office. Mr. Goddu, the math teacher, made his special chili, someone else brought a nice loaf of bread, another teacher got drinks, and I was in charge of decorations. I made sure that everyone got custom-made Thanksgiving hats with hand turkeys on them. The room was decked out in homemade ridiculous decorations that looked like Buddy the Elf had come for dinner. The meal was magnificent. It was a wonderful step out of the ordinary, and it gave the staff special time and space to enjoy one another's company. That spring, on the opening day of baseball season, we did it again. We grilled hotdogs and decorated and watched the opening inning of the Philadelphia Phillies game, all during our uninterrupted lunchtime.

If I hadn't lived this situation, I'd be thinking the same thing as many of you: my school would never let that happen. They grilled hotdogs at school? Shouldn't you be working since you are on school time? Must be nice to have such freedom! The thing is, the fun we had that year made all of our classes better. It gave everyone the energy to try out new ideas in class. It helped us laugh more, which made helping difficult students easier. Although we shared all of those magical moments together, that year was just as stressful as any other. A student was shot that year. Another kid was arrested in the hallway as the other students watched. We had to deal with just as much heartbreak and disappointment as any other year. The difference was that we made an effort to not stay in that place of brokenness. My guess is that many toxic teachers weren't born that way. At some point, they thought this job would be great. They wanted to serve the students and make their classes exceptional. Somewhere along the way, they lost their spark and grew miserable. For some teachers, there will be nothing you can do to make their day better. It's as if you are offering them a gift and they are refusing to take it. You can flip that idea, however, and make it work for you. If a colleague offers you a gift of anger, resentment, or aggravation, you can choose not to take it. Choose joy and peace instead. Here is a list of ways to make your day awesome despite the naysayers.

Consider making a friend. Everything is better with friends. Put your radar up and look for someone who's fun and who cares deeply about the work and the mission. Then ask them to get a drink or coffee after school. If after school is no good, invite them to your house some night for ice cream or dinner. Remember the relationships that you tend are the relationships that grow. C. S. Lewis once said, "Friendship is born at that moment when one person says to another: 'What! You, too? I thought I was the only one.'" It is important to find people, even if it's only one or two, with whom you can share both your successes and your frustrations. It will make all the difference.

Be accessible. Every day between classes, I stand in the hallway and talk to my good friend Mr. Hasty. His door is right next to mine. We joke with the kids as they walk by and make our hallway the silliest in the school. Hasty is a great guy to check in with when I am feeling low. We also get to share whatever hilarious or unexpected awesomeness happens in our classes. Just having those few moments of shared joy or frustration helps before I walk into my next class. It's important to leave your classroom now and again and to remember you are part of something bigger than your class. It is life-giving to spend the five minutes between classes with someone who is enjoyable to be around.

Say hi to people. I say hi to everyone I pass—teachers, administrators, students, the nurse, the maintenance guys, everyone. Every once in a while, you'll encounter someone who doesn't want to say hi. They snub you or pretend they don't hear you. When that happens, I use an old tip from one of my heroes, Pat Croce, the former owner of the Philadelphia 76ers. Pat says when someone tries to ignore you, you need to give them the "sonic boom" hello. Don't give them the simple head nod and say, "What's up?" in a barely audible voice. Instead loudly give them the greeting they deserve: "WHAT'S UP, MY FRIEND!" No one can ignore you when you sonic boom them. It's too much love all up in your face! Side note: Please understand that I'm talking about people who are purposely ignoring you because they can't be bothered to say hello. Be sensitive to quiet or introverted people who are friendly in their own ways and might be hurt or intimidated by the sonic boom.

Make breakfast together. Last year our vice principal surprised the staff by bringing in a waffle iron and making waffles for us in the office. Everyone came in during their prep periods and enjoyed waffles, fruit, coffee, and juice. It was a great way to disrupt the daily routine and inject some fun into an otherwise regular day.

Surprise people with kindness. When my fuel light comes on and I need to make a coffee run in the afternoon, I regularly grab a second or third cup of coffee for someone else. Without fail, as I walk back into the school building, some teacher will see me and say jokingly, "Hey, is that for me?" My answer is "YES! It is for you, my friend." You can also drop it off to a teacher in need and make their day a little better.

Share your appreciation. Every so often, Ms. Flounders, one of the sweetest people I work with, will write cards to her co-workers. It's a wonderful surprise to get a handwritten card telling you that you are awesome. That little act goes a long way. I've gotten a few cards from Flounders over the years, and I keep them in my desk drawer to read on days that are overwhelming.

Let people know you care. I was once absent from school for a week because of a heartbreaking family situation. It was the kind of thing that made it hard to show up for classes the next day. When I walked into my room, my friend Pelletier had transformed the back wall of my classroom into an enormous "Magical Garden" mural that he and the kids decorated. It had an eight-foot-tall dragon with my head on top. It had garden gnomes and butterflies and all manner of ridiculousness. It was over-the-top and absurd and perfect. To be surprised by the outrageous kindness of others is one of life's great joys. What an incredible difference it made for me to walk into my classroom that day, to turn on the lights, and to be surprised by the kindness and thoughtfulness of others.

Be strategic in your associations. Just as in the game Battleship, it's all about strategy! I have actually never played that game, but I've seen the commercial, and I think the metaphor holds up. Anyway, I never walk into a meeting, luncheon, or professional development session without surveying the scene first. I always pause at the entrance and quickly look over who's there and where they're sitting. I want to put myself at the table that's going to be a party. If it's a professional development meeting I'm interested in, I want to put myself with people who will get pumped too. If I know that we will be working in groups, I make sure I am with people who are hard workers. If I want to laugh, share good stories, or help someone to feel connected, I put myself in that environment.

Infuse a spirit of play into your school's culture. Several years ago, the head of our school's English department, Mr. Ribay, asked if all of the teachers would come to school on Halloween dressed as the cast of the sitcom *Parks and Recreation*. Everyone agreed, and it was a hit. Think about how much your students lose their minds when you show up to school after getting a haircut. Now imagine what would happen if you came to school dressed as their favorite comic book character or movie star. Not only did we create a fun disruption in the daily lives of the kids, we also came together as a team and did something fun together. School can be so serious and repetitive. It's of the utmost importance to be able to laugh with one another. Since that Halloween, our English department has raised the bar every year. We've come to school dressed as the cast of *Game of Thrones*, the characters from Nintendo's *Mario Kart*, the cast of *The Walking Dead*, and our favorite Will Ferrell characters. Every year, the students fall to pieces, and I get to teach class like Luigi or Little Finger. It's a win-win.

DRESSING UP LIKE MARIO AND LUIGI FOR HALLOWEEN

Invite people to be a part of your awesomeness. A few years ago, I invited a guy named DJ Cosmo Baker to come in and show the students in my History of Hip-Hop class how to mix and scratch on the turntables. We turned the speakers up to eleven, and the students took turns deejaying while other kids took turns freestyling over the live beats. As the period went on, teachers from surrounding classrooms and even office staff began walking into our room to see what in the world was going on. They loved it! Everyone wanted to be a part of what was happening, because no one wants to be left out of a

DJ COSMO BAKER TEACHING KIDS TO MIX AND SCRATCH

good party. When you're doing something fun, inspiring, or exciting in your class, invite others to share in the magic. In perhaps the most formative book of my life, *Into the Wild*, Christopher McCandless, comes to the realization just before dying that "happiness is only real when shared." Don't celebrate in a vacuum. Shoot a faculty email or text before you have the best class of the day, and let others share in what you and your students have created.

REAL RAP:

REMEMBER HOW MUCH POWER YOU HAVE

All schools have their share of toxic teachers, people who will trash your ideas and talk behind your back. When you face that, it's important to remember how much power you have. While others use their power and influence to spread gloom and doom, you have the power to make someone else's day and make your school an exciting place where you and others want to be. Maybe some of the ideas I've listed here are things you can immediately implement, and perhaps some of them are not possible at all in your school. Don't get hung up on the specifics. If your school has a policy saying faculty aren't allowed to come to school dressed like Ron Burgundy or King Koopa . . . well, it is what it is. The bigger question is what *can* you do? Accept the challenge, and try to think of ways to shine some light on the days and lives of others. Even with the level of freedom I'm allowed at my school, I still have dozens of ridiculous ideas I haven't been able to implement . . . yet. For instance, I have a dream to build a reading loft in my classroom. I essentially want a treehouse in my classroom for students to read and do work in. You would have to climb a ladder to get to the top and use a sliding board or firefighter's pole to get down at the end of class. It would have nooks to read in and bean bags and cushions to sit on, and it would infect the classroom space with magic and fun—kind of like if Willy Wonka had a place to read in his chocolate factory. I can hear what you're asking already. "Reynolds, why would you go to all the trouble and spend so much money to build something so ridiculous?" Great question. The answer: because it is awesome. What kid wouldn't want to climb a ladder to a classroom treehouse to read and think? I haven't been able to make this dream a reality yet, but that doesn't mean I'm going to just throw my hands in the air and give up. Instead I accept the challenge and think of other ways to make school fun in the meantime. What are ten ways you could make this school year the best ever? Really. Write them down. If you could get away with anything, what would it be? Fill someone's office or classroom with balloons. Surprise a colleague with confetti and streamers on their birthday. Have secret dance parties on the elevator. Write someone a thank you card. Bring someone flowers.

9
LETTER TO A YOUNG TEACHER

Dear New Teacher,

After all of those years of college, practicums, student teaching, certification tests, and job interviews, when you walk into the classroom on that first day of school, the students will not care that you showed up to teach them. Despite what you've heard in college and seen in movies, they are not sitting in class with their hands folded just waiting for the right person to show up so they can be all they can be. They won't care about your classroom decor or your super fun ice breaker. The students won't care if you dressed cool or if your hair's on point. They won't care that you love hip-hop and comic books too. They won't care if you taught in Africa or if you are married to the love of your life. Most of your students won't want to read any of the books that you picked or that are a part of the curriculum. They won't care that you care, that your life has had hard times too, and that you remember what it was like to be a teenager. No one cares that you come into school at the break of dawn and stay up late to prep for tomorrow, that you are running on four hours of sleep a night because you are writing the most thorough lesson plans ever. It doesn't matter to them that the classroom rules and procedures have been clearly posted around the room and your syllabus has been carefully crafted to answer every question on the first day of school.

The students will still talk when you stand in front of the class, even when you tell them you'll wait. They'll talk after you repeatedly tell them how important this assignment is. They will talk when you are in the "zone of proximity." You might get cursed out and have someone threaten to "fuck you up." Few other teachers will celebrate your small classroom victories, and most won't come in to make sure things are okay. When you and your students create something epic, no one else will care. Except for that one lunch lady. She loved it, and she will give you extra chicken nuggets at lunch. No one will willingly hand over their time, respect, or effort just because you came to teach them.

What *will* happen is your students will ask for your respect, and when given, you will earn theirs. If you take the time to explain *why* an assignment is important and take the time to reverse-engineer how it will make them better, they *will* do it. That kid in the back of the class who told you to "go fuck yourself" is waiting to see how long it takes you to give up so he doesn't have to live through another disappointment. You'll buy that kid lunch, find out what his story is, and listen without feeling like you need to fix him. You will learn that your attention is more important than your advice. You will try to be the teacher you always needed, the teacher you always dreamed of being. Sometimes you will win big, but more often than not, you will fail. You will learn to take the punch to the mouth, spit the blood out, and keep going. The following year, more students will come in and do their best to make your life miserable. Buy them lunch and learn their stories.

Stand at the front door of the school every morning, shake every hand that walks into the school, and say hi to everyone, especially that six-foot-five, two-hundred-fifty-pound kid who refuses to look at you. The same thing goes for the girl who walks down the hallway only looking down, wears socks on her arms, and has more eye makeup than Alice Cooper. Make her know you see her. Everyone wants to be seen—just not everyone wants you to know it. Show up every day. Take the rules off the wall. Leave the procedures. Make your classroom a place of wonder and safety for all students. Laugh with your students. Read with them. Eat with them. If they bring in some food you never heard of that their mom made and carefully placed on tin foil for you to try, eat it. It will taste like appreciation. You will have no magical powers over your class, and no one is coming to help you or save you. *You* need to make the class you want.

Ask the kids what they want to learn. Buy them books they want to read. Have cereal parties because pizza parties are boring. Eat cereal with the least nutritional value. If you're on a budget, get Top Ramen. That stuff is six packages for a dollar. Celebrate birthdays with silly string. Remember that fair is not equal. Don't act like ESL, dyslexia, ADHD, and other such challenges are a choice. Have an after-school fiesta complete with snacks and music to help the ESL kids catch up. Help the kid with dyslexia know he's not broken. Remind him that he is perfect the way he is, and get that dude an audiobook. And for all those kids who can't sit still, give them a job, a standing desk, and some room to move.

Dear teacher, your first year in the classroom will be the hardest thing you've ever done. There will be little immediate gratification. Just remember that you are in the business of planting seeds. Some of those seeds will grow fast and bloom furiously. Some will grow so slowly that you'll only notice the changes when you take time to compare where they are to where they started. Some will never grow in your garden at all because it's simply not their time or their place. And some will grow like bamboo. Their roots will develop for years underground and will look like they are going nowhere until one day they rocket up and almost overnight become what they were meant to be.

Remember that you are not in this alone. Look around your school for like-minded educators to partner with and create something awesome. If you look around and don't see anyone who is your same kind of crazy, then look online. Swarms of teachers all over the world are already doing what you so badly want to do. Remember, success leaves clues. Figure out what those teachers are doing that works, and take it back to your own classroom.

Remember, there are no silver bullets in education. You will need to teach like a DJ. Sometimes you will have the perfect lesson at the perfect time and the kids will love it, and other times you will get punched in the stomach with the reality that your efforts have fallen short. In those moments, you can never give up. Smile in the face of your fear, and simply change the record as many times as you need to until you find the right jam that gets everyone out of their seats and dancing again.

Remember that you can only teach great when you feel great. Put time, energy, and love into yourself first. Fill yourself up so you can give abundantly.

On those days when you want to call it quits and look for a different line of work, sit quietly and remember why you started teaching in the first place. Was it because someone inspired you to follow in their footsteps? Was it for your community? Was it to stand in the face of injustice? Let that feeling flood your heart. Let it pour gasoline on your fire. No one started teaching so they could have kids crush it on the test or fulfill all of the curriculum standards. They started because they wanted to create magic in the classroom and make kids excited about education.

Remember to remind your kids every day that you care about them. That they are perfect just the way they are. That they are enough, and that no matter what they've been told by the world, they belong everywhere.

Remember this job was never about us. Education is always only about the kids. You are enough. Go teach your class off.

Peace,

APPENDIX: REYNOLDS'S RESOURCES

My Online Presence

Website: realrapwithreynolds.com
YouTube: youtube.com/channel/
UCRGA_FqyigEPmh5U37Yn7fA
Instagram: instagram.com/realrapwithreynolds
Facebook: facebook.com/realrapwithreynolds
Facebook Group: facebook.com/groups/566468247135630
Twitter: twitter.com/realrapreynolds

People I Admire

Father Gregory Boyle
Website: homeboyindustries.org/our-story/father-greg/
Books: *Tattoos on the Heart*
G-Dog and the Homeboys

Derrick Brown
Websites: writebloody.com
brownpoetry.com

Rafe Esquith
Website: hobartshakespeareans.org
Books: *Teach Like Your Hair's on Fire*
There Are No Shortcuts
My interview with Rafe: youtu.be/jpYZcyLZ5ag

Tim Ferriss
Website: tim.blog

David Goggins
Website: davidgoggins.com
YouTube: youtube.com/watch?v=dIM7E8e9JKY

Phil Hansen
Website: philinthecircle.com
Ted Talk: ted.com/talks/phil_hansen_embrace_the_shake
discussion

One Fab Teacher
YouTube: youtube.com/channel/UCoI9taX-A8LsmZkApOl_ylw
My interview with One Fab Teacher: youtu.be/bUZ9RTOtDTQ

Ouigi Theodore
Website: thebkcircus.com

Gary Vaynerchuk
Website: garyvaynerchuk.com
Video from our first visit: youtu.be/EGw1FRfHmnc
Video from our second visit: youtu.be/BiLMNQo-Wso
My videos about meeting Gary Vaynerchuk: youtube.com/
playlist?list=PLuyHiKIP4CyicsxKsrh2bLGSoCoG7bsg8

Books That Fill Me with Hope and Get Me Excited about the Day

The Bible
The World According to Mister Rogers by Fred Rogers
I Feel Great and You Will Too by Pat Croce
Wisdom of the Ages by Wayne Dyer
Tribe of Mentors by Tim Ferriss
Tribes by Seth Godin
You Can't Hurt Me by David Goggins
The Seven Storey Mountain by Thomas Merton
The Way of the Heart by Henri Nouwen
Crazy from the Heat by David Lee Roth
The Hawk and the Dove series by Penelope Wilcock

Podcasts I Recommend

Aubrey Marcus Podcast
Design Matters with Debbie Millman
The Ed Mylett Show
The GaryVee Audio Experience
Impact Theory
Jocko Podcast
Joe Rogan Experience
The Rich Roll Podcast
School of Greatness
Short Story Long
Tim Ferriss Show
The Tony Robbins Podcast

Artists and Creators Who Have Had a Positive Impact on My Classroom

Amberella
Website: amberellaxo.com

Thomas Campbell
Website: thomascampbell-art.com

Dallas Clayton
Website: dallasclayton.com

Jimmy DiResta
Website: jimmydiresta.com

Andy Goldsworthy
Website: artsy.net/artist/andy-goldsworthy-2

Phil Hansen
Website: philinthecircle.com

Oliver Jeffers
Website: oliverjeffers.com

Max Joseph
Website: maxjoseph.com

Alloyius Mcilwaine
Website: alloyiusmcilwaineart.com

Casey Neistat
Website: caseyneistat.com

Alexandre Orion
Website: alexandreorion.com

Mac Premo
Website: macpremo.com
YouTube: youtu.be/orPcjXPT14Q

Isaiah Zagar
Website: phillymagicgardens.org

ACKNOWLEDGMENTS

More than anyone, I want to thank my wife-for-life, Jenni, who has been my partner in all of life's adventures since the senior year of high school. You are the most wonderful friend and wife I could have ever hoped for.

I'd also like to thank my offspring, Brody and Marley. You two are the most precious blessings I've ever received. Every room gets brighter when you walk into it. It is because of you that the YouTube channel, *Real Rap with Reynolds*, and this book ever came to be.

To Mom and Dad, I miss you, and I so wish you could see the life your boy has been blessed with.

To my family and friends near and far, I am who I am because of your love and support. Thanks for being such a tremendous source of love and fun.

To my friend Adam Welcome, it was your phone call telling me, "Dude, you've gotta write a book," that got this project moving. If we are indeed the average of the five people we hang with the most, I have upped my game by becoming friends with you.

To Alex Kajitani, you have been a great mentor these last few years, and I appreciate all of the time you spent answering my many phone calls, texts, and emails. You have given me the courage to share my teaching and life experience and helped me to remember that our ordinary can be someone else's extraordinary.

To all of my students, this book would never have happened unless you had given me your trust in and out of the classroom. It has been my honor to be in the classroom with you. Remember, no matter what anyone else tells you, you belong everywhere.

Finally, to God, you have loved me into being and I am eternally grateful.

ABOUT THE AUTHOR

CJ Reynolds has never won an award for teaching, but he has made a boat out of a single piece of plywood, run every day for an entire year, made two human beings, and taken his students on a metric ton of adventures, including climbing temples in Belize, ziplining and hiking volcanoes in Costa Rica, and spray painting graffiti in the back alleys of Philly.

CJ teaches high school literature and the History of Hip-Hop in West Philadelphia. He is also the creator of *Real Rap with Reynolds*, a YouTube channel aimed at giving viewers an authentic glimpse into what it looks like to teach high school in inner city Philadelphia while, at the same time, helping both novices and veterans be the educators they have always dreamed of being. CJ's real rap teaching philosophy is simple: in the classroom, relationships are king, and the job of a teacher is always only about the students.

Along with sharing his real-world approach to teaching on YouTube and hosting his Sunday night live show, *Sunday Night Teacher Talk*, Reynolds also has a popular Facebook page, Real Rap with Reynolds Teacher Talk, where educators from around the world gather to share ideas and give each other support. CJ also mentors

new and veteran teachers, and travels around the country sharing his message with teachers. These resources are available via his website, which is listed in the appendix.

CJ is the father of two children, Brody and Marley, and the husband of one wife, Jenni. When not in the classroom, he can be found with his dog, Bentley Chewbacca Sam Elliot Reynolds, working in his garden or in his tiny woodshop.

INVITE
CJ REYNOLDS
TO YOUR NEXT
PROFESSIONAL
DEVELOPMENT EVENT

Speaking Topics

Teach Your Class Off

Don't wait to be the teacher you've always dreamed of becoming! In this session, we will cover some of the most difficult topics educators attempt to navigate and how they can take their classrooms from surviving to thriving, from creating student engagement, to building strong student/teacher relationships, to classroom management, to time management, and more. New and veteran teachers will learn practical skills that they can implement immediately to help them teach their class off.

Teach Like a DJ

How do we engage students when each year our classes have different needs and learning styles? Like any good DJ, teachers need to be able to read a room and know their crowd. Anything can be taught once you have a captivated audience. In this session, we will discuss how to gain an understanding of how our students learn best and how to create wildly engaging lessons that will make your students want to come to class and become a partner in their own learning.

How to Build Enduring Student Relationships

Knowing how to build positive student relationships is the key to any successful classroom. Strong relationships help minimize classroom management issues and create a positive school culture. In this session, we will work through how to get to know your students and their learning styles so they can have the most successful year possible in your classroom.

Real-World Social Emotional Support for Students and Teachers

Learning how to implement social and emotional support for your students can be a far cry from actually implementing it in your classroom. In this session, we will work through best practices for teachers and their teams that they can immediately put into place in their classrooms to help their students and colleagues through trying emotional times.

Classroom Management

Strong classroom management provides students with a structured safe environment in which they can learn and grow. In this session, we will discuss how teachers can figure out what classroom management styles and strategies are best for them and their students. Teachers will leave able to immediately implement a number of tried-and-true strategies in their classrooms to help students have a successful year.

Preventing Teacher Burnout

All teachers have times when they feel burned out. Finding ways to reenergize your classroom, your lessons, and yourself is essential to having a successful year in the classroom. In this session, educators will learn strategies to help bounce back from burnout and to have the best year ever in their classrooms.

If you're interested in hiring CJ to speak on any of these topics for your school, district, or event, please contact him via his website, realrapwithreynolds.com.

MORE FROM DAVE BURGESS Consulting, Inc.

Since 2012, DBCI has been publishing books that inspire and equip educators to be their best. For more information on our titles or to purchase bulk orders for your school, district, or book study, visit **DaveBurgessConsulting.com/DBCIbooks**.

More Leadership & School Culture

Culturize by Jimmy Casas

Escaping the School Leader's Dunk Tank by Rebecca Coda and
    Rick Jetter

From Teacher to Leader by Starr Sackstein

The Innovator's Mind-set by George Couros

It's OK to Say They by Christy Whittlesey

Kids Deserve It! by Todd Nesloney and Adam Welcome

Let Them Speak by Rebecca Coda and Rick Jetter

The Limitless School by Abe Hege and Adam Dovico

Next-Level Teaching by Jonathan Alsheimer

The Pepper Effect by Sean Gaillard

The Principled Principal by Jeffrey Zoul and Anthony McConnell

Relentless by Hamish Brewer

The Secret Solution by Todd Whitaker, Sam Miller, and
    Ryan Donlan

Start. Right. Now. by Todd Whitaker, Jeffrey Zoul, and
    Jimmy Casas

Stop. Right. Now. by Jimmy Casas and Jeffrey Zoul

They Call Me "Mr. De" by Frank DeAngelis

Unmapped Potential by Julie Hasson and Missy Lennard

Word Shift by Joy Kirr

Your School Rocks by Ryan McLane and Eric Lowe

Like a PIRATE™ Series

Teach Like a PIRATE by Dave Burgess
eXPlore Like a Pirate by Michael Matera
Learn Like a Pirate by Paul Solarz
Play Like a Pirate by Quinn Rollins
Run Like a Pirate by Adam Welcome

Lead Like a PIRATE™ Series

Lead Like a PIRATE by Shelley Burgess and Beth Houf
Balance Like a Pirate by Jessica Cabeen, Jessica Johnson, and
   Sarah Johnson
Lead beyond Your Title by Nili Bartley
Lead with Culture by Jay Billy
Lead with Literacy by Mandy Ellis

Technology & Tools

50 Things You Can Do with Google Classroom by Alice Keeler
   and Libbi Miller
50 Things to Go Further with Google Classroom by Alice Keeler
   and Libbi Miller
140 Twitter Tips for Educators by Brad Currie, Billy Krakower, and
   Scott Rocco
Block Breaker by Brian Aspinall
Code Breaker by Brian Aspinall
Google Apps for Littles by Christine Pinto and Alice Keeler
Master the Media by Julie Smith
Reality Bytes by Christine Lion-Bailey, Jesse Lubinsky, and
   Micah Shippee
Shake Up Learning by Kasey Bell
Social LEADia by Jennifer Casa-Todd
Teaching Math with Google Apps by Alice Keeler and
   Diana Herrington
Teachingland by Amanda Fox and Mary Ellen Weeks

Teaching Methods & Materials

All 4s and 5s by Andrew Sharos
The Classroom Chef by John Stevens and Matt Vaudrey
Ditch That Homework by Matt Miller and Alice Keeler
Ditch That Textbook by Matt Miller
Don't Ditch That Tech by Matt Miller, Nate Ridgway, and
    Angelia Ridgway
EDrenaline Rush by John Meehan
Educated by Design by Michael Cohen, The Tech Rabbi
The EduProtocol Field Guide by Marlena Hebern and
    Jon Corippo
The EduProtocol Field Guide: Book 2 by Marlena Hebern and
    Jon Corippo
Instant Relevance by Denis Sheeran
LAUNCH by John Spencer and A. J. Juliani
Make Learning MAGICAL by Tisha Richmond
Pure Genius by Don Wettrick
The Revolution by Darren Ellwein and Derek McCoy
Shift This! by Joy Kirr
Spark Learning by Ramsey Musallam
Sparks in the Dark by Travis Crowder and Todd Nesloney
Table Talk Math by John Stevens
The Wild Card by Hope and Wade King
The Writing on the Classroom Wall by Steve Wyborney

Inspiration, Professional Growth & Personal Development

Be REAL by Tara Martin
Be the One for Kids by Ryan Sheehy
Creatively Productive by Lisa Johnson
The EduNinja Mind-set by Jennifer Burdis
Empower Our Girls by Lynmara Colón and Adam Welcome
The Four O'Clock Faculty by Rich Czyz
How Much Water Do We Have? by Pete and Kris Nunweiler
P Is for Pirate by Dave and Shelley Burgess
A Passion for Kindness by Tamara Letter
The Path to Serendipity by Allyson Apsey

Sanctuaries by Dan Tricarico
Shattering the Perfect Teacher Myth by Aaron Hogan
Stories from Webb by Todd Nesloney
Talk to Me by Kim Bearden
Teach Me, Teacher by Jacob Chastain
TeamMakers by Laura Robb and Evan Robb
Through the Lens of Serendipity by Allyson Apsey
The Zen Teacher by Dan Tricarico

Children's Books

Beyond Us by Aaron Polansky
Cannonball In by Tara Martin
Dolphins in Trees by Aaron Polansky
I Want to Be a Lot by Ashley Savage
The Princes of Serendip by Allyson Apsey
The Wild Card Kids by Hope and Wade King
Zom-Be a Design Thinker by Amanda Fox